You Wretched Corinthians!

You Wretched Corinthians!

The Correspondence between the Church in Corinth and Paul

Hans Frör

SCM PRESS LTD

Translated by John Bowden from the German *Ach Ihr Korinther! Der Briefwechsel der Gemeinde in Korinth mit Paulus*, published 1994 by Christian Kaiser Verlag/ Gütersloher Verlagshaus, Gütersloh.

0 334 02597 4

First British edition published 1995
by SCM Press Ltd, 26–30 Tottenham Road,
London N1 4BZ

Typeset at The Spartan Press Ltd,
Lymington, Hants
and printed in Great Britain by
Biddles Ltd, Guildford and King's Lynn

Contents

v

Preface

In the year 50, around twenty years after the arrest and execution of Jesus of Nazareth, Paul came to Corinth with his message of the risen Christ. He worked there for eighteen months with his two colleagues Silvanus and Timothy. A lively church, composed of people from very different backgrounds, grew up, filled with the spirit of the new life. In spring 52 Paul left the young Christian movement to its own resources and spiritual gifts and went with his colleagues to Ephesus.

In 55 Paul received disturbing news that led him to write a letter to the Christians in Corinth. This gave rise to a lively correspondence; for the problems were not solved by the first letter, but developed into a stormy conflict.

We owe an important part of the New Testament, Paul's letters to the Corinthians, to these events. Amounting to twenty-nine chapters in all, they are the most comprehensive correspondence in the Bible. They contain replies, letters of self- defence, requests, desperately polemical letters and vigorous personal reactions to news from Corinth, both in letters and by word of mouth.

In the New Testament we find only half the correspondence: the letters which Paul wrote. But in them he refers so often to the news from Corinth that we can't help imagining the other side as we read them. It's like listening to someone on the telephone: we can't hear the person on the other end of the line, but what he or she is saying is reflected in the words of the speaker we can hear. We can infer some things from his or her words, but some things we have to guess, and some things remain enigmatic to us, so that we have to ask what was actually said at the other end.

In this book I've attempted to let both sides have a say: Paul with his passionate letters, *and* the Christian men and women of Corinth with their questions and views, their conflicts and rivalries, their accusations and insults, their enthusiasm and bluntness, their euphoria and their crises. That has produced a two-way correspondence: the Christian men and women of Corinth write to Paul, and Paul writes to the church in Corinth. I've taken Paul's letters from the New Testament and attempted to translate the original Greek text into a language which can be understood today. I've inferred, reconstructed or invented the letters of the people of Corinth from the texts of Paul.

To understand Paul and to get to know the Corinthians, I've used works of theological and historical research, and I've summarized the most important features of this research in the appendix (137ff.). The notes (164ff.), to which references are given in the main text, contain further information about the relevant passages and indicate the dividing lines between what is historically certain and what has been invented. Three maps of the city of Corinth in the time of Paul (187ff.) set the scene. Finally, in the appendix there are some suggestions for those who want to make practical use of this book.

I've also felt it important to give readers with an interest in the subject some information about the theoretical background of my work. But I hope that the correspondence is immediately acessible even without any of these explanations. That was my aim: to arrange the texts of Paul and the letters from the Corinthian church which go with them in such a way that they can be read and experienced as a story without any further comment.

I'm grateful to all those who have supported me in this work. My thanks to Christian Dietzfelbinger for exegetical comments and encouragements, to Bernard Wolf for advice and information about phenomena of ecstatic piety and to Hans Gerhard Behringer and Barbara Herrmann for reading the manuscript in an unfinished state and giving me valuable suggestions about its final shape.

Easter 1994
Hans Frör

Introductions

The people

Very different kinds of people met together in the church of Corinth. There were parties and groups, social contrasts, and differences arising from cultural and religious origins. To depict this variety it has been necessary to introduce a large number of characters.

In the following list different type-faces distinguish what is historical from what is fictitious. Everything based on historical information from the New Testament is printed in *italic*; the other names, occupations, ages, etc., have been invented.

The way in which names are written has been assimilated to the language-area from which they come. This is meant to give a better impression of the mixture of languages and peoples in Corinth. Here are some guidelines:

Roman-Latin women's names end in –a ('Fulvia'), Greek names in –a ('Xenia'), –e ('Chloe') or –is ('Chrysallis'). For Jewish women I have chosen names from the Old Testament ('Deborah', 'Esther').

Roman-Latin men's names end in –us ('Fortunatus'), Greek names in –os ('Achaikos'), –as ('Stephanas') or –es ('Sosthenes'). I have also given Jewish men Old Testament-Hebrew names ('Boaz', 'Jonah') where they do not have Greek names (like Krispos).

In names of Greek origin ph is written instead of f (Greek 'Phalakros', Latin 'Fulvia').

Paul, Peter, Timothy, Ephesus and Corinth have been left in their familiar forms.

All the people mentioned here are Christians, so the designation 'Jewish' or 'Jew' stands for 'Jewish Christian' members of the church. 'Gentile Christians' are described in terms of their origin ('Romans', 'Greeks', 'foreigners'). 'Godfearers' were attached to the Jewish community as Gentiles before their baptism, without having to submit to the whole law.[1]

People in Corinth

Achaikos (= *'from Achaia'*), fifty-six, a Greek slave, chief steward of *Stephanas, I Cor.16.17.*

Boaz, fifty-three, a Jewish cattle-dealer who has immigrated with his family from Syria. He comes from a church founded by Peter.

Chloe, fifty, a Greek businesswoman with trade connections in the East.[2] A widow. *Her people inform Paul about how things are in Corinth, I Cor.11.*

Chrysallis (= 'butterfly pupa'), thirty-five, a mirror-polisher, a former slave owned by *Gaius*, now freed by him. She still works in his business.

Deborah, twenty-eight, a Jewish slave, a musician.

Erastos, forty-four, *Greek*, a freeman,[3] *a Corinthian city official. Rom.16.23; II Tim.4.20.* Married to a non-Christian wife.

Esther, thirty-eight, Jewish, a newcomer, who works with her husband Mattat in a pottery.

Fortunatus, twenty-six, nephew and 'right-hand man' of *Stephanas*, son of a Roman legionary, *I Cor.16.17.*

Fulvia, thirty-seven, a free Roman trader, a godfearer and widow with children who are almost grown-up.

Gaius, fifty-two, *a free Roman citizen, who owns a* bronze foundry and *a spacious villa which is available for meetings and for guests of the church*. A widower. *I Cor.1.14; Rom.16.23.*

Hannah, fourteen, a Jewish girl, grand-daughter of *Krispos*.

Jonah, seventeen, son of Boaz, Jewish.

Karylla (= 'little nut'), sixty-six, Armenian slave, housekeeper to *Gaius*.

Krispos, sixty, *a Jew, who before his baptism was president of the synagogue*. Runs a food store with his family. *I Cor.1.14; Acts 18.8.*

Leah, thirty-one, a free Jewish midwife, married to a non-Christian Jew.

Lykos (= 'wolf'), around forty-five, a slave imported from abroad, a port worker.

Mara, forty, an Arab slave, a barmaid in a pub in the western harbour.

Mattat, forty-six, a Jewish freeman, a newcomer, works with his wife Esther in a pottery.

Melas (= 'black'), fifty, a newcomer, an Egyptian freeman, a godfearer, a private teacher, single.

Nannos (= 'dwarf'), about forty. A slave of unknown origin owned by the shipbuilding business in Corinth, a specialist in construction.

Oknos, twenty-nine, a freeman from Cyprus, single, works as a cook in the theatre tavern.

Phalakros (= 'bald-head'), twenty-seven, a Greek freeman, single, without a proper job.

Phoibe, forty, *a Greek business woman, a leading church worker ('deaconess')*[4] *in the church at Kenchreai, Rom.16.1.*

Phrygis (= 'from Phrygia'), nineteen, a slave, works in a hair-dressing salon in the city centre.

Quartus (= '*the fourth*'), thirty-six. A freeman, a haulage contractor with a young family. *Rom.16.23.*

Rufina, twenty-five. A seamstress, free, of Roman origin, Timon's wife.

Stephanas, a Greek freeman, a vintner, forty-five, a godfearer. *Achaikos* and *Fortunatus* work in his vineyard, *I Cor.1.16; 16.15,17.*

Tertius (= *'the third'*), forty-seven. A freeman, a secretary in the provincial administration of Achaia. Church secretary. *Paul dictates his letter to the Romans to him: Rom.16.22.*

Timon, thirty-three, a Greek freeman, book-keeper in the Corinthian tax office, husband of Rufina.

Titius Justus(= *Titius the Just*), *a Roman freeman, a godfearer,* fifty-eight. Shoemaker. *His house is next to the synagogue. Paul lived there. Acts 18.7.*

Xenia, thirty, a Greek freewoman, wife of a non-Christian architect.

Zinga, an African slave, about twenty-four, housemaid in a Roman household.

There are discussions about a man from the church whose name is not mentioned, I Cor.5.1–5.

People outside Corinth

Apollos, a Jewish-Christian theologian who studied in Alexandria (probably with Philo). An independent apostle, working alongside Paul in Ephesus. Also active in Corinth around 53; Acts 18.24; I Cor.1–4.

Aquila, see Prisca.

Barnabas was sent with Paul and Titus in 48 as a delegate of the Gentile-Christian community of Antioch to Jerusalem, to the 'Apostolic Council'. Paul worked with him for a long time, until they fell out in the dispute between Peter and Paul (in Antioch, 48/49). From then on they carried on separate missions. Acts 13–15; Gal.1; 2,1–9; I Cor.9.6.

The brothers of the Lord. According to Mark 6.3, Jesus had four physical brothers: James, Joses, Jude and Simon. I Cor.9.5. See James.

James led the community in Jerusalem with Peter and was later its sole leader; with Peter and John he was involved in the discussions at the 'Apostolic Council' (48) and received the collection brought by Paul (56). Acts 15.13; 21.18; Gal.1.9; 2.9 + 12; I Cor.15.7.

Paul (= 'the little one'), with the Jewish name Saul, a Jew from Tarsus, a tent-maker, a Pharisee. He studied Jewish theology in Jerusalem, was a bitter opponent of the young Christian community and persecuted it. Called to be an apostle around 33 by the risen Christ, he first worked in Damascus and Arabia, and then as an apostle in the church of Antioch. From there he was sent with Barnabas and Titus in 48 to the 'Apostolic Council' in Jerusalem (Gal.2.1–10; Acts 15), where an agreement was reached which gave the Gentile mission freedom from the Jewish law. At the same time he committed himself to arranging a collection for the church in Jerusalem. A little later, differences of opinion over relations between Jewish and Gentile Christians led to a dispute in Antioch (Gal.2.11–21): Paul clashed not only with 'some people from James' and Peter but also with Barnabas. Thereupon he detached himself from the church in Antioch and began an independent mission with new colleagues (Silvanus, Timothy, etc.). In autumn 50 he arrived in Corinth and worked there for eighteen months, until spring 52. Then he went to Ephesus. From there he wrote the letters to the Corinthians in 55. Paul is now presumably around fifty-five.

Peter: Cephas = 'rock' (Aramaic) = Petros (Greek) = Petrus (Latin ending). Simon Peter was the first disciple of the earthly Jesus, and was initially leader of the earliest church in Jerusalem. Later, he carried on a mission in Syria and probably also reached Rome. He was one of those involved in the discussions at the Apostolic Council (48). A little later Paul had a vigorous argument with him in Antioch about eating with Gentile Christians. Some scholars conjecture that Peter also visited Corinth, but probably the statements on which they base their view simply mean that Christians from his communities came to Corinth and there proclaimed their allegiance to Peter. Matt.16.18; Gal.1–2; Acts 15; I Cor.1.12; 3.22; 9.5; 15.5.

Prisca and Aquila, a Jewish Christian couple, tent-makers, who had been expelled from Rome and settled in Corinth shortly before Paul arrived there. Paul initially lived and worked with them. They went to Ephesus at the same time as Paul. A church met in their house there. I Cor.16.19; Rom.16.3; II Tim.4.19; Acts 18.2; 18.36.

Silvanus, called Silas in Acts, is a colleague of Paul's. Paul founded and built up the church in Corinth with him and Timothy in 50/52. Acts 15.22–18.5; I Thess.1.1; II Thess.1.1; II Cor.1.19.

Sosipatros, also called Sopatros, is a fellow-worker from Beroia in Macedonia who according to Acts 20.4 was delegated to take the collection and in Rom.16.21 sends greetings from Corinth. I have supplied his name in the gap in the text in II Cor.8.22, cf. Tychikos.

Sosthenes is mentioned as a fellow correspondent in I Cor.1.1. It is uncertain whether he is the president of the synagogue in Corinth who according to Acts 18.17 was beaten before the tribunal.

Timothy (Timotheos), son of a Jewish Christian mother and a Greek father (Acts 16.1), has been Paul's closest and most constant colleague since 49. Paul got to know him when moving towards Europe. Since then he has been uninterruptedly at Paul's side or on journeys for him. Paul mentions him as a colleague at the beginning of almost all his letters. Paul founded and built up the church in Corinth with him and Silvanus in 50/52. At least once he sent him from Ephesus to Corinth. From Acts 16 on; I Cor.4.17; 16.10; II Cor.1.1 + 19.

Titus, a member of the church in Antioch, was with Paul as one of the 'uncircumcised', i.e. a representative of the Gentile Christians, at the 'Apostolic Council', where the collection for the 'poor' in Jerusalem was agreed. Titus later took special responsibility for arranging this collection: Gal.2.1-13; II Cor.2.13; 7.6–14; 8.6–23.

Tychikos is a colleague of Paul's from Ephesus, who is 'sent' by Paul to various churches and according to Acts 20 is one of those bringing the collection. Acts 20.4; Col.4.7; Eph.6.21; II Tim.4.12; Titus 3.12. I have inserted his name in place of the deleted name of the 'brother' who according to II Cor.12.18 was with Titus in Corinth and to whom according to II Cor.8.18 Paul and Titus hand over the organization of the collection (cf. also Sosipatros).

Christians travelling through Corinth, itinerant preachers and apostles, remain anonymous.

The city

At the time of Paul, Corinth was a Roman metropolis.[5] The Romans had destroyed the old Greek Corinth in 146 BCE. Shortly before his murder (44 BCE), Julius Caesar had the city rebuilt for Roman settlers. A monumental city centre in the Roman style was constructed. With its countless shops, markets, business streets and adminstrative buildings, even today Corinth is still recognizably a key trading port (see the map, 'City Centre, Excavations', 189).

Corinth owed its importance to its geographical situation on the Isthmus, between the seas. Land traffic between the Greek mainland and the Peloponnesian peninsula had to pass over a narrow strip of land less than four miles wide, and east-west shippers could save a voyage of several hundred miles if they took their cargoes over the Isthmus. The loads were transported between the two great harbours, Lechaion in the west and Kenchreai in the east. Small ships could be towed along the 'Diolkos', a paved slipway at the narrowest point of the Isthmus where the canal now cuts through the land (cf. the map 'Isthmus of Corinth', 190).

As a crossroads of trade routes, Corinth was stamped by world trade in the way that London, New York or Frankfurt are today. A well organized state adminstration made wide-ranging trade links possible. Immense riches could be gained not only by people with inherited possessions but also by the up and coming, for example former slaves who had been freed. Cultural and sporting organizations (the Isthmian games every two years) made Corinth an international rendez-vous for well-to-do society. The work was done by male and female slaves, who, despite their lack of freedom, at any rate had a degree of security. In addition there were casual labourers who earned the basic minimum and could suddenly find themselves unemployed, since the labour market was volatile. Economic contrasts also developed beween the city and the country. The population in the province was poor, and capital was concentrated in the city.[6]

The social level of the population tended to become higher, the further out into the country people lived. The old Corinth extended over three areas: above, on the sloping plain between the city centre and the rocky mount of Akro-Corinth, lay the villas of the rich with their gardens. The huts of the transport workers must have clustered down below, by the harbour. In between were presumably people with an intermediate social status, including new arrivals (cf. the map 'The City of Corinth', 188).

Mobility throughout the Mediterranean brought a large number of nations and cultures, and an equally colourful mixture of religions from East and West, into the city. The recognition of this plurality was a matter of survival. At the same time people became increasingly sceptical about this world, which functioned and yet was unpredictable. Many of them felt strangers in it and sought guidance from the various esoteric cults on offer. Not only people and goods from all over the world came through the crossroads at Corinth; wisdoms, religions and cultic practices from every corner of the globe were also 'traded' there. Faith in Jesus Christ had to prove itself in competition with them. Moreover, even within the young church, different groups competed with and against one another. So not only philosophers, preachers, teachers of salvation and miracle workers of all kinds appeared in Corinth, but a whole variety of Christian apostles and missionaries were continually coming and going. Paul was one of them.[7] From the perspective of the people in Corinth he was one of many who had come to this great city with their teaching and had founded a religious association, just one among many others. In those days he certainly didn't have the undoubted, unique status which he has today as apostle to the Gentiles and author of biblical writings. What he was and how important he was had to emerge simply from his message and what he did.

The Correspondence

Tertius, secretary of the church in Corinth, Achaia

to

Paul the apostle, now in Ephesus, Asia[1]

God be with you!

Dear Paul, the church has commissioned me to write the enclosed letter to you. What an impossible task! How can anyone do justice to this community in a letter? Set all its spirit and life down in pen and ink?

I expressed my hesitations and made counter-proposals. For example, Stephanas or Krispos or Chloe or some other sister or brother could dictate the whole letter to me in a quiet hour. Two or three people could compose a letter much better than everyone together in a large gathering. But no, it was said that the letter had to come from the whole church. And of course it had to present a faithful picture of the feast. You, Paul, were to share in our experience of the fullness of the spirit as you read it, just as though you were in our midst. Impossible! I protested to the end. But it was no use. Stephanas clapped me on the shoulder in his confident way and said, 'Well, Tertius, you can do it. Just write down everything that the brothers and sisters say to you.' Just write everything down! Easy for him to talk. Everything that the brothers and sisters say! Not to mention that much of what for example the port workers, kitchen helps, household slaves or drovers say has first to be translated into proper Greek; they often speak in a wild and disorderly way, so that it's quite impossible to get down everything they say. I'm one of the fastest stenographers in the provincial administration and often get called on to take

I

the minutes at difficult conferences. But this gathering was far beyond anything I had been expected to do before.

The result confirms my fears. What was to have been a letter is now more like the minutes of a stormy session. The sounds of enthusiasm and jubilation in Christ are more restrained, while the discords of petty disputes seem all the more urgent. In the final version I get the impression that the letter consists almost entirely of squabbles and nagging. Perhaps that kind of thing flows more quickly from my pen than joy in the spirit. The result is a dangerously distorted picture – when we really wanted to invite you to join in our celebrations. I'm sorry, but I can't change anything now. Tomorrow Chloe's people are getting on board ship and taking our letter with then. Chloe is sending them to Syria and Egypt to tidy up some business, and they have to start on the first ship of the spring.[2] They will change ships in Ephesus. Moreover this business trip was the occasion for writing to you. We planned it long ago, last autumn, when Titus and Tychikos[3] came to visit us. They kept putting it off, and now it's suddenly got to be done like lightning.

I've written a few more remarks to you in the letter, about some brothers and sisters whom you don't yet know. Many of them only came to us in the last three years, after your departure. The disciples of Apollos keep talking as though it made no difference at all in the fellowship of Christ who one is in worldly society, what one does, and whether one belongs to anyone or is free. But I recall that you often also enquired about what people did in the world, so I wanted to introduce at least some of them to you. I hope that reading this doesn't disturb you too much. Really the letter is pretty confusing as it is.

Greetings from me, Tertius. God's blessing be with you!

The church of God[4] in Corinth, Achaia

to

Paul the apostle, and all working with him, in Ephesus, Asia

'The grace of Christ be with you and the power of his spirit!' Stephanas has hardly dictated the heading than interruptions come tumbling in: 'Write him that he must come!' 'Paul, we need you!' 'Look what's become of us!' They all keep interrupting one another, particularly of course the old gang who owe their deliverance to you. Stephanas attempts to sum up what he's hearing, but the brothers and sisters keep going one better in calling out what I'm to write. It's impossible to get it all down.

'You must visit us, Paul!' Stephanas is speaking once again. 'We've missed you for too long. It's almost five years since you brought us the message of Christ. You and Silvanus and Timothy, and then you left us and since then we haven't seen you. You must come and see us, us, your saints[5] of Corinth. You must see what the beginnings have turned into. You would be absolutely delighted, and we could share your enthusiasm and together praise God that the sound unites with the music of the universe and fills heaven and earth.' Everyone joins in loudly, clapping their hands.

'But as we don't know when you will see us again, if at all, we've decided to write to you so that you can at least celebrate wth us from afar. As usual, we're meeting in Gaius' home on the Lord's day, sitting here packed so closely together that the chill evening air, which is coming into the hall through the open courtyard,[6] is almost pleasant. You know Gaius' villa and how roomy it is. But as we are now, when everyone meets the place is hardly big enough, and we grow more numerous week by week. So here we are together and are including you in our prayer, imagining that you are singing the song with us.'

Now Nannos stands up to sing his song.

[Nannos, the 'dwarf', one of the slaves from the shipyard. You will certainly recall this short, stocky man. For almost a year he sat regularly, but hesitantly, on the visitors' bench, fascinated and suspicious at the same time, and then, when you were about to go, the Spirit suddenly seized him and he asked for baptism from you. You yourself weren't able to baptize him, but nevertheless, more than almost anyone else he is one of yours.]

There he stands, little Nannos from the shipyard, and begins to sing, or rather shout, his song. He utters the words not in a fury, but enthusiastically, like hammer blows, and his rhythm draws everyone in, first the port workers and the transport

3

slaves, the kitchen helps and the cowgirls, and then all of us. We join in his song:

> Jesus is Lord,
> you are the Lord,
> no one but you.
> All those who still
> boss us around,
> will bow the knee,
> Lord before you.
>
> Though they may sneer,
> trample me down,
> smothered in filth,
> though they may make
> money from me,
> treat me as dirt,
> vain as they are,
> patronize me,
> humble and hurt,
> nothing can touch me.
> You are the Lord,
> Jesus alone.

Mara leaps up, singing with her whole body.
[Mara from the harbour pub: she comes from Arabia; the landlord bought her years ago as a young girl.]

Mara takes up the song, adding her own verse, and anyone with eyes to see can see how the song moves her:

> Jesus is Lord,
> you are the Lord,
> no one but you,
> All those who still
> boss us around,
> will bow the knee,
> Lord, before you.
>
> Though they may use me,
> prey to their lusts, toy to their whims,
> cheap entertainment for guests;

4

though they rip out
what grows in me,
children aborted,
torn from the womb,
Jesus my Lord, it's over, over –
Jesus my Lord, stabbed in the belly,
O how it hurts,
as if today.

You will disarm them,
you are the Lord,
Jesus alone.

The women around Mara shout 'Yes' and 'Amen', and even the curious and interested visitors on their benches are obviously moved. Some even join in the song, which Nannos now sings again.

Amen.
Jesus is Lord,
you are the Lord,
no one but you.
All those who still
boss us around,
will bow the knee,
Lord before you.

Gods they may put in the heaven above,
there in the temple, on stands in the squares,
stony expressions of power that's too great,
constant control from eyes that are cold,
bend upon keeping our souls under foot,
lies and deceit
come from the priests.
Nobodies they,
you are the Lord,
Jesus alone.

Deborah has taken up the song with her flute and rejoices before Christ with her instrument, and Phrygis has an inspiration, exults and sings, seized by the Spirit:

Jesus alone,
Lord of all Lords,
even the least
are in your eyes
greater than they.

[Phrygis is a young girl, almost still a child, but her exuberant faith has already attracted many. Her owner has a hairdressing saloon by the temple of the Julians and she works there. Xenia is one of those she's won over, a better-class woman. Xenia was sitting in the chair, and Phrygis, standing behind her, saw her face in the mirror and suddenly had a prophetic inspiration: 'No meaning, no aim, no commitments, no risk,' she said, her hands in Xenia's hair: 'You want to find life, but you're numbing yourself.' No one had ever said anything like that to Xenia. It touched a nerve. That's Phrygis. And Xenia is now one of us: she's meanwhile come to interpret the holy scriptures better than some Jews.]

The song has come to an end and all are silent. However, in the corner where the disciples of Apollos are, someone bends over Melas and whispers in his ear – loud enough for me to understand: 'Remarkable, Nannos and his song. A bit of polishing and it could be a poem.' I don't know whether Nannos could hear it; he was sitting on the other side, wrapped up in himself, and didn't stir.

Stephanas uses the silence to dictate another couple of sentences.

'That's how it is with us, dear Paul; that's how we begin our meetings. And we all feel that you're with us in your prayers and that you've now sung the song of praise with us in the spirit. See what's become of us – and we owe it all to you.'

'Others were also involved,' Melas has interjected this remark. [Melas, the black-eyed Egyptian, baptized by Apollos and his most ardent pupil. In ordinary life he has set up as a private teacher.[7] Evidently he's anxious that not enough respect is being paid to his great master.]

'Write that to him,' he tells me, and dictates, backed up by the cries of all the followers of Apollos, 'After you, respected Paul, Apollos came.'

'He came because Paul sent him.' That was an interruption by Nannos, evidently offended at the whispering of the Apollos clique. He looks agitated. Undeterred, Melas continues:

'The church of Ephesus sent Apollos. With a letter and a seal.[8] And Apollos came at just the right time. He brought what the community had hitherto lacked, wisdom. I don't mean the shallow sayings of itinerant philosophers.[9] Apollos taught us wisdom as a way of the gospel, as a method of preaching Christ, as a medium of understanding between the cultures, something that speaks to everyone from Egypt to Rome. There is nowhere better than Egypt for studying this kind of wisdom.'[10]

'We bow to the Egyptians and their mighty wisdom,' mocks Mara, and wins laughs from the other women from the port area. But Melas the Egyptian isn't put off his stroke:

'Indeed, Apollos our apostle studied the holy scriptures in Alexandria, among the most famous theologians in the world, among the most austere philosophers on earth, and learned to interpret them as a source of the spirit and truth, as a reflection of the divine radiance . . .'

Now Fortunatus, Stephanas' nephew, comes over to me, looks over my shoulder at my notes, and asks, 'Tertius, are you writing all this down?' He then turns to Melas and says, 'Look, stop going on about Apollos and his brilliance as though Paul didn't know him. They're both working in Ephesus and Paul probably knows him better than you do.'

Melas keeps cool. 'What Apollos taught us was essential for the church. He opened the doors to the educated and influential people in the city. Erastos is an example of that: respected Paul, did you ever manage to win over such a high official from the city administration? And Erastos in turn made some of his colleagues curious, so that some now belong to us. Apollos also resumed dialogue with the Jews in the synagogue, after it had been completely blocked under your leadership.'

'You can't blame Paul for that,' intervenes Krispos. 'When I was still president of the synagogue he spoke regularly with us, and the vigorous disputes didn't frighten him. It was only when I left the Jewish community and came over to the Christian church, bringing many Jews and even more godfearing[11] Gentiles with

7

me, who are now all here among us, that they understandably became bitter, and Paul could no longer appear in the synagogue. That was that!'

'Be that as it may,' Melas continues, 'Apollos opened the door again to constructive discussion, with wisdom and passion. And on an amazing number of issues he in fact succeeded in bringing people closer together theologically. It was only on the question of the Messiah that he made no progress. Nevertheless, relations with the synagogue have become more relaxed, and there have been no more beatings, as there were before your departure.[12] Certainly he would have managed to convince some people from the synagogue had he been able to stay with us longer.'

'He went when his model pupil began to surpass his teacher in wisdom and eloquence,' mocked Fortunatus. 'With all due respect to the qualities of your Apollos, we are and remain Paul's community, and we're proud of it.'

'With all due respect to your Paul . . . I belong to Apollos!' counters Melas, and his friends approvingly support him.

Then Mattat and Esther his wife stand up. He puts his arm around her and says, 'We belong to Christ.' No one quite understands that, and I too think, 'What does that mean? Do they want to lecture the church? Don't we all belong to Christ? Or do they want to be special saints, more closely bound to Christ than the rest of us?'

[No one knows very much about Esther and Mattat. They came to us last year, a childless couple, who work in a pottery in the north of the city. Since then they've constantly been at meetings, but don't say much. Some find their restraint a lack of spirit, others find it arrogant. People don't get on with them. However, if anyone is sick and needs care or practical help, they're there, Esther above all, but also Mattat.]

Melas keeps standing there with admirable self-control, untouched by the stir around him. He points his finger at me as a sign that I'm to go on writing and says, 'I value the work of Apollos, Paul, and I'm saying so not to put you down but to bear witness that the saints of Corinth stand on a solid foundation. Two truly significant apostles founded the church, you and Apollos. That needs to be pointed out. For some of the people who come here want to demote us to a second-class

8

community. It would be wrong to allow this, and in any case it's the real reason why we wanted to write to you.'

'That's right,' says Stephanas, and picks up the thread. 'There's some uncertainty among us. Preachers keep coming through Corinth; they visit us, speak God's word to us, are our guests, and then they go on. We gladly welcome them, because they increase our faith and bring news of other churches and other apostles. To begin with we were amazed that they were quite happy for us to pay their expenses. You hadn't prepared us for that approach from you. You always earned your own living and rejected our hospitality.'

'That was no fault of mine!' Titius Justus held up his hands beseechingly. 'He lived with me for a year and more. For a year and more I tried to persuade him, but it was no use: he didn't want any gifts. No bed, no food, no drink. He could have had it all from me free, he and Silvanus and Timothy too. It was no fault of mine. Now I'm regarded as someone who made a business out of God's message.'

'What disturbed us,' Stephanas continued, 'were the remarks made by our guests when the subject of hospitality came up. They thought it suspicious that you earned your own living, saying that this was unseemly for a true apostle. One of them remarked: "He must have had his reasons. A true apostle has a right to hospitality." Another even remarked indignantly: "Why does he scorn what Jesus himself ordained? Didn't Jesus forbid the apostles to take more with them on their way than a staff –no bread, no purse, no money, no second coat? Didn't he say, 'The labourer is worth his food'?[13] Has this Paul who calls himself an apostle so little confidence that the Lord will open the doors to him?" One man remarked that he had travelled around a lot as a preacher and had felt everywhere that Paul's churches were a bit too close to their founder and uncritical of him. However, he could understand that, since Paul, this ex-Pharisee from Tarsus, indeed impressed people. That's how these people talk; they spread uncertainty and then move on. Of course we defend you as well as we can. But surely you can understand how such remarks puzzle us?

Finally some Jews came from Syria, from churches which Peter had founded. They told us of the disagreement between

9

you and Peter, how you fell out with each other in Antioch and remarked that in any case that Simon Peter was the greatest, and far more significant than you, Paul, because he was the first to see Jesus after his resurrection and had known him and gone around with him during his earthly life. So anyone who belonged to Peter was on firm ground.'

Boaz interrupts Stephanas [Boaz, a cattle dealer, is an immigrant from Syria who has brought his family with him. He is one of the Jews who came to us from the Peter churches. Peter himself baptized him, and all the members of his family. He tends to emphasize this on every possible occasion.] He waves both arms to get a hearing and then says: 'Please, I must make it quite clear that this isn't about the vanity of a few immigrant Syrian Jews, but about a fundamental decision of the Christ himself. He called Simon, his first disciple, "Cephas" – Petros, rock, for those among you who don't understand Hebrew.[14] And Cephas isn't a nickname or a pet name, but a title. Cephas, the rock, towers above all and is the foundation on which the Lord is building his community. So Simon is the rock. Not Apollos and not Paul, whether you like it or not. "You are Cephas, and on this rock foundation I shall build my church." Please, that's not our invention. It's a saying of the Lord.'

'Paul, you mustn't be afraid that we're doubting you,' Nannos calls out through the general muttering. 'We're not allowing ourselves to be blown around by such talk. But we need you to provide some clarity. Please come, Paul! Show them who you are. Take a ship, and you can be here next week.'

'You'll have a long wait. He won't come.' This remark and the laughter which follows come from the corner where the admirers of Apollos are gathered. Or was it Onkos? It would be just like him.

'We've formed an investigating committee,' Erastos now declares with the businesslike approach of a city official. 'We must get to the bottom of the accusations. The question is simply how we can show that you're a legitimate representative of the gospel and that we are therefore a legitimate community. We've already made welcome progress in our research, but it would best for you to appear before the committee in person. We've already questioned Titus and Tychikos, your colleagues; we did that when they visited us in the autumn. Titus in particular was a valuable witness, because he'd been involved in the negotiations in Jerusalem. So he was able to confirm to us that you had been discussing responsibilities there, you and Barnabas, with the key apostles in Judaea, and also with Simon whom they call the Rock. He told us that you officially agreed, with a handshake, that Cephas should work among the Jews and you among us Greeks. This agreement already puts us on solid ground. He said that you committed yourself to raising money for the brothers and sisters in Jerusalem.[15] We can all bear witness that you're certainly working hard at that. And we're glad to help: Titus didn't have to spend long asking us for a contribution. We won't leave the poor in Jerusalem in the lurch. But these irritating suspicions about you must be removed. The meeting with the apostles in Jerusalem is seven years in the past, and some things have happened in the meantime. We need your comments. If you can't or won't come, put them writing, so that we can settle the matter.'

By now it's late, and Mara has begun to lay the table for the meal. Guests and onlookers are excluded, and we begin the supper, include you in our thanksgiving, remember that at this very moment you are celebrating the supper in Ephesus, perhaps in Prisca's and Aquila's house, at the same table as us. Some people remember that Titus mentioned dangerous threats against you and pray God to protect you and keep you alive. Then, after the Maranatha,[16] Chrysallis begins to sing.
[Chrysallis is an inspired singer who was baptized by Apollos. In everyday life she works as a mirror-polisher[17] in Gaius' bronze foundry. She belonged to Gaius; he freed her when she was baptized, but she's remained in his business.]
Chrysallis sings:

Wisdom I speak
in the group of the perfect,
mystery of God.
No eye has seen it,
no ear has heard it,
up it arises out of the depth.

Wisdom pervades me,
light in a mystery,
fire of the spirit.

Spirit sees all things
depths of the Godhead,
I see in the spirit.

I disclose wisdom,
filled with the spirit,
teach to enthusiasts
spirit experience.
We can grasp all things,
if grasped by the spirit,
but it can't be grasped.

That's Chrysallis' song, and it sounds as though she were no longer on this earth. While she is still singing, Melas, the black-eyed Egyptian, echoes her words. All the formality, the coolness, the control, drops from him like a strait-jacket: he joins in her song in higher tongues, and with him others, men and women from among the followers of Apollos. They sing in tongues,[18] and it sounds like the angels singing in delight at God's glory. And Deborah accompanies the fiery breath of the spirit on her flute, while little Phrygis keeps singing words from Chrysallis' song with her bell-like voice:

Wisdom pervades me,
in the fiery spirit,
I praise God.

When it's all gone quiet and everyone is sitting enrapt, seized by God's nearness, Quartus says to me, softly, but loud enough for some to hear: 'So who belongs to the group of the perfect? All of us here? Or Apollos' people? Or those who can sing like Chrysallis, Melas and Phrygis?'

'The one who is perfect knows it,' Melas instructs him. 'Wisdom makes itself known.' And when he notices Quartus' uncertain look he adds: 'Don't worry if you're doubtful. It may be that you aren't there yet. There are stages as in earthly human life. First we're children, immature and innocent; we need to be educated by the experienced, and if we can't take things in solid chunks, like the educated, we still sit at table with them.' And Melas points at Mara and the others serving the supper.

Quartus is silent. Not, however, it seems to me, because Melas' answer has satisfied him.

After the supper Krispos says the blessing and most people now leave; only a few continue to crowd round me, want to add their greetings and bits of news about those you know. Gaius, our host, greets you longingly. He lost his wife this winter. She died of a painful fever, and our prayers couldn't save her. She was so weak that she couldn't even be baptized. Gaius was baptized for her vicariously after her burial.[19] That was a comfort for him. We also had to bury Deborah's mother. Timon and Rufina are mourning their son. He was still very little, couldn't get any air, and died. Fulvia has been mourning her husband a long time – more than two years now. He'd intended to be baptized, but Fulvia had to receive baptism in his place. Now she's sick, getting thin, can hardly eat anything, can't keep anything down. A number of people have fallen ill over the winter and they worry us. Zinga the African visits them whenever she's free, but it's no use. She's helped many of us with her healing powers, but here they don't work. We can't understand why. There's nothing for it but for us to help to look after them. Esther is tireless in the houses of the sick, doing what she can. If you were with us, Paul, the sick would blossom into fresh life. You must visit us!

Greet our brother and friend Sosthenes,[20] your fellow-worker. We know that he's a good advocate for us, like Prisca and Aquila, our brother and sister. Greet them all, and all their people. Greet Timothy and Silvanus, to whom we owe much, and of course also Apollos.

All those who know you, greet you. So do I, Tertius, the scribe.

We bless you. The riches of the grace of our God be with you!

Paul, apostle of Christ Jesus, called by God's resolve, and Sosthenes, the brother

to

the church of God in Corinth, and those who have been made holy in Jesus Christ, called as saints

We greet you, with all who everywhere call on the name of our Lord Jesus Christ, among you and among us: Grace to you and peace from God our Father and the Lord Jesus Christ.

I keep thanking God on your behalf for the grace which God has given you in Christ Jesus. You've become rich in him in every respect, rich in speaking, rich in knowing; the testimony to Christ has put down powerful roots in you, so that you don't lack any of the gifts of God. You're well equipped as you move towards the revelation of our Lord Jesus Christ! He will strengthen you to the end, so that no one will accuse you on the day of our Lord Jesus. God is faithful! Through him you've been called to the fellowship of his son Jesus Christ, our Lord.

However, I do beg you, dear brothers and sisters,[21] in the name of our Lord Jesus Christ, to see that you all pull together. Don't let there be any splits among you, but stand ready with the same views and the same attitude. Chloe's people have told me that there are disputes among you. What I mean is that each of you says 'I belong to Paul', 'I belong to Apollos', 'I to Cephas', 'I to Christ.' Is Christ then divided? Was Paul perhaps crucified for you? Were you baptized in the name of Paul? I'm grateful to God that I didn't baptize any of you but Krispos and Gaius, so that no one would get the idea that you were baptized in my name. Oh, and I also baptized the family of Stephanas and perhaps others – I'm not quite sure now. For Christ didn't send me to baptize but to communicate the gospel. And that not with a wisdom of words, so that the cross of Christ isn't watered down. For talk of the cross is nonsense to the lost, while for us who are saved it's the power of God. For it is written:

'I will destroy the wisdom of the wise,
I will devalue the reason of the reasonable.'

14

Where are they, the philosophers, the theologians, the intellectuals of this world? Hasn't God made the world's wisdom stupid? Certainly! For originally the world was embraced by God's wisdom. Nevertheless, it didn't grasp God's wisdom. Therefore God resolved to save believers by the nonsense of the message. And that's what's happening now:[22] Jews are looking for proofs, Greeks are calling for wisdom; but we're making known the crucified Christ. For Jews he's a slap in the face, for citizens of the world nonsense; but to those who are called, both Jews and Greeks, Christ is the power of God and the wisdom of God. For the nonsense of God is wiser than human beings, and the weakness of God is stronger than human beings.

Brothers and sisters, take a look yourselves at all those who are among the called: not many wise and educated people by ordinary standards, not many influential people, not many from good families. But God has sought out the less well educated in society to put the educated to shame, and God has sought out the weak on the fringe of society to put the strong to shame. God has sought out those who haven't had a chance from birth, those who've been written off by society, who are nobodies, to remove from power those who are someone – so all humanity has nothing to be proud of before God.

He is the source of your being; you *are* through him, you *are* in Christ Jesus,[23] whom God has made wisdom for us – and justification, and sanctification, and redemption. What has been written is true now:

'Let him who boasts, boast of the Lord!'[24]

Take the way I came to you, brothers and sisters. I didn't come with any great eloquence or wisdom when I proclaimed to you the mystery of God. For I had resolved to know nothing among you but Jesus Christ, the one who was executed, So I appeared among you weak and anxious and indeed often trembling; my speeches and my sermons didn't carry conviction through educated words. But they proved effective in the spirit and in power – so that your faith should be rooted not in human wisdom but in the power of God.

On the other hand, we do speak 'wisdom in the group of the perfect'! However, this is not a wisdom of this age or of those in power in the world, who are passing away. No, we speak 'the wisdom of God in a mystery', wisdom which is hidden, which God predestined for us before all time to be a light for us, which none of the rulers of this world have known. Had they known it, they wouldn't have executed the Lord of light. But as it is written,

'No eye has seen it,
no ear has heard it,
what has not arisen
in any human heart,
what God has prepared
for those who love him.'

Indeed, God has disclosed this through the spirit. For 'the spirit sees all things, even the depths of the Godhead'.

What person can know that – who can know what moves people? Only the human spirit which is in them. So, too, no one has understood what moves God, but only God's spirit itself. That is what we have received. Not the spirit of the world, but the spirit which comes from God himself, that we may 'see' what God has given us.

And we speak of that not with words which human wisdom teaches, but with those which the spirit teaches: thus 'we teach to enthusiasts spirit experience'. No human beings grasp with the capacities of their own souls what moves the spirit of God. It's nonsense to us; we can't understand it, because it can be grasped only by the spirit: 'We can grasp all things if grasped by the spirit, but it can't be grasped.' For

'who has understood the mind of the Lord
so as to be able to advise him?'

What we have is the mind of Christ![25]

However, I couldn't address you, brothers and sisters, as those with experience in the spirit. I had to talk to you as ordinary people, as children in Christ. I gave you milk to drink, and not yet solid food, since you couldn't have taken it. Even now you can't take it, since in fact you're still quite ordinary people. For where jealousy and disputes prevail among you, aren't you behaving just like ordinary people? When one person says, 'I belong to Paul' and another 'I to Apollos', aren't you all human? What is

Apollos? And what is Paul? They've received commissions through which you've come to believe. And each of them has performed the task assigned to him by the Lord. I planted, Apollos watered, but God gave the increase. So it doesn't matter who plants or who waters, but rather who gives growth: and that is God. The one who plants and the one who waters are equal. Each will receive his reward, depending on his work. So we are God's fellow-workers: you are God's planting, God's building. With the grace of God which has been given me, like a skilful master builder I laid the foundation. Someone else is building on it. But each must look how he is building. No one can lay another foundation than the one which has already been laid: Jesus Christ. Now if anyone builds on the foundation, whether gold, silver, precious stones, wood, hay or straw, it will become evident what he has constructed. The day of God will demonstrate this, for God will reveal himself with fire. The fire will show what a person's work is made of: if what someone has built remains standing, he will profit. If someone burns down his work, he will lose everything. He himself will be saved, but as it were through the fire.

Don't you know that you're God's house, that God's spirit dwells in you? If anyone damages God's house, God will damage him, for God's house is holy, and that is what you are.

No one should have any illusions. If someone among you thinks that he is a wise man of this age, he should become a fool so that he becomes truly wise. For the wisdom of this world is nonsense with God. For it is written of him that he

'catches out the wise in their own plots',

and later,

'The Lord sees through the thoughts of the wise, so that they come to nothing.'

So don't let anyone use the respect of others as a foundation. Everything belongs to you: Paul, and equally Apollos and Cephas, the whole world, life and death, present and future. Everything belongs to you. But you belong to Christ, and Christ belongs to God.

That's how you should regard us: as workers for Christ, as stewards of the mystery of God. And of course stewards are expected to be trustworthy. Therefore I see no reason why I should answer to your investigating committee or to any other human authority.[26] I don't even pass judgment on myself. I'm not aware of anything I've done wrong. But that isn't what acquits me. The Lord is my judge. So you, too, shouldn't judge anything prematurely, before the Lord comes. He will also bring to light what is hidden in darkness, and uncover the deepest motives. Then everyone will receive recognition from God.

Brothers and sisters, I've cleared up all this about myself and Apollos so that you can learn by our example not to get above yourselves,[27] not to encourage one another to support a particular leader. Who put you on a pedestal? What do you have that you haven't received? And if you did receive it, why do you suggest that you didn't receive it? Evidently you're already full, already very rich. Evidently the kingdom of God has already begun without us! If only you really could already rule in God's kingdom, so that we could rule with you! That would be splendid! For it seems to me that God presents us apostles as the last act of all in the world theatre, as candidates for death. We provide a grim spectacle for angels and men. We do – the stupid ones for Christ's sake, while you are the wise ones in Christ. We're weak, but you're strong, You're splendid, and we're without honour. To this very moment we're hungry, thirsty, torn apart, maltreated, with nowhere to settle, exhausted by the work that we do with our hands. People taunt us – and we bless. People persecute us – and we remain. People use bad language about us – and we comfort. We've become the garbage of the world, everyone's rubbish, and still are at this very moment.

I'm not writing this to shame you, but because I want to make you think, since you're my offspring and I love you.[28] Even if you had a thousand teachers in Christ to bring you up, you don't have many fathers. I brought you into being in Christ Jesus, through the gospel. So I beg you, follow my example. That's why I'm also sending Timothy to you, whom I love and on whom I can rely, and who is my offspring in the Lord.[29] He will remind you how I present and teach the things of Christ everywhere, in every church.

Some people puffed themselves up, suggesting that I won't come to you. But I'm coming to you soon, when the Lord wills, and I shall take note, not of the chatter but of the power of these puffed-up people. For God's kingdom doesn't consist in chatter but in power. Which would you prefer? For me to come to you with a whip or with love and a tender spirit?

What's more, we hear that there's adultery among you, a kind of adultery which one doesn't find even among the Gentiles: one of you has his father's wife. Are you puffed up about that, instead of regretfully dissociating yourselves from the one who has done such a thing? I may not be there in person, but I am in the Spirit, and I at any rate have already decided, as though I were there in the name of the Lord Jesus, that the one who has done this – so when you're gathered together and I'm with you in the Spirit with the power of our Lord Jesus, then, I've decided to deliver over the one who behaves like this to Satan for the destruction of his earthly existence, so that he himself is saved on the day of the Lord![30]

It isn't good for you to show off. Surely you know that a little leaven leavens all the dough! Clean out the old leaven, so that you may become new dough, since that's what you really are. You're 'unleavened', for our passover lamb has been slaughtered – and that is Christ. So let's celebrate the feast,[31] not with the old leaven, not with the leaven of wickedness and malice, but with the unleavened bread of clarity and truthfulness.[32]

Greet Nannos the shipbuilder and Mara the sister for me, and all those who confess Christ as Lord. Greet all the brothers and sisters with the holy kiss![33] Greetings to you from the churches in Ephesus. The grace of our Lord Jesus Christ be with you!

Tertius, secretary of the church in Corinth, Achaia

to

Paul the apostle in Ephesus, Asia

Peace be with you!
Dear, esteemed Paul, your letter caused a great stir and some argument, especially the end, and led the thoughtful ones in the

church immediately to write you this answer, which I've just prepared and am sending to you. The letter was composed by a group of brothers and sisters on behalf of the whole church in the dawn of the passover. Timothy had advised this, since the arguments had become heated and threatened to disturb the peaceful ending of the festal worship. We had baptized[34] twenty-six new brothers and sisters and wanted to celebrate the supper with them.

Of course there were also arguments in the group which wrote the letter. I hope that nevertheless I've succeeded in reproducing the points of dispute and the different positions properly. Our letter might give the impression that your letter and Timothy's arrival only caused squabbles. That certainly wasn't the case. We were delighted when we heard that Timothy had landed in Kenchreai. Anyone who could get off work went to meet him, and when he showed us your letter, we could hardly wait for the meeting. It arrived at a good time, since we were just preparing for the passover. Indeed, we were celebrating the new passover for Jews and Gentiles, which you've celebrated with us twice. The first time, four years ago, I wasn't yet there. That must have still been in Stephanas' vineyard, in a small group, but I often think back to the second time, shortly before you left us. That's how we also celebrated the passover of Christ, yesterday, the feast of the coming of the risen Christ who redeems us from the slavery of the powers of heaven and earth. And the twenty-six newly baptized brothers and sisters were living signs of the passover, which includes all people. There were only a few from the earthly Israel: two Jewish widows and a young bank employee from the synagogue congregation, but many Greeks, Romans and foreigners from every corner of the earth: a young lady from Cyrene who had been brought on a trip by a businessman; a Spanish sailor stranded here, too disabled to be signed up; a Roman officer and his family, including a bright-eyed tutor whom he probably got hold of in a raid on the northern provinces; several women slaves from the households; freemen seeking to build a new life here. The whole world was present in this group being baptized. Not only did Israel go through the water into freedom, but all were saved for life in Jesus Christ by God's mighty act. It was a passover without frontiers. And in it you yourselves could proclaim the gospel – 'the power of God and the wisdom of God for Jews and Greeks'! We looked forward to that. And when Achaikos picked up your letter and began to read, the tension was evident to all.

Perhaps expectations had been too high. The brothers and sisters reacted in different ways, and not just at the end of the letter. Quite soon Lykos, one of the port workers, interrupted the reading and called out: 'What's all this talk about marginal groups and uneducated people? Where are we, then? Haven't we all gone through the water into the holy land? There are no longer slaves and freemen here! There are no longer Jews and Greeks! No longer male and female![35] Didn't we say and sing this again today with the new brothers and sisters when they came up out of the water? I praise God that I'm no longer a nobody! Not here. Why is he pushing us back into the stinking muck from which we came? Or are only the rich holy?'

Xenia tried to back up Lykos and added her own thoughts, probably thinking that she was striking the same note. Yes, it was abundantly clear that people shouldn't be talking about all that here, especially when children were present. She had always forbidden her little ones to say the word 'cross' or to taunt their playmates by calling them 'cross-fodder'[36] – Xenia clearly found it difficult to utter this word. Such talk wasn't allowed in her family, and so far she'd always kept the children away from executions.

But then Nannos intervened, shouting out: 'Those crosses aren't made for you ladies and gentlemen, and the people who are being tortured to death don't hang between your terrasses. The crosses are put up for the likes of us, and there they stand, down there where we live, to the right and left of the main roads. In the early morning the children creep out of the huts and see them hanging there; they go to work on the plantation between these executed men.'

So it went on, to and fro, while Achaikos was reading out your letter; it's not unusual to have a conflict of opinion during worship. Some people had something to say, like Melas, who read sharp attacks on Apollos between the lines of your letter;[37] some kept their mouths shut, like Boaz, when he heard that there is no other foundation than Christ. Chrysallis went wide-eyed in bewilderment when she heard her own words echoed, and Erastos shook his head as if to say, 'All right, we won't' at the way in which you turned down him and his investigating committee. Some people then remarked that they had over-reacted. And when Achaikos read our your summing up, 'All things belong to you and you belong to Christ', Esther was suddenly seized by the spirit, directly and to everyone's amazement, since hitherto we had found her rather reserved. However, now she expressed her joy by speaking in tongues. It was a foreign language for most people, but these were bright, clear, happy sounds, between laughing, weeping and singing, and more than all these. Others joined in, competed in speaking in tongues, and Deborah turned Esther's enthusiasm into music on her flute, as if she were going in front of everyone through the water into the new land, into the midst of the life of the risen Christ. Erastos, who has the capacity to make sense of such speaking and singing, translated what he understood.

'Christ is free!
Nothing can force us.
All is ours
since we are Christ's.'

He noted down the whole song and we've put it at the beginning of our letter. You'll read it and see it: we celebrated passover, the passover night of the living Christ, with you and your letter.

Your letter seemed to come to an end, and some people were already beginning to prepare the meal; then came that addition at the end, that thunderbolt which no one had really expected. As I've said, it put the whole church in a turmoil. Quartus in particular was beside himself. 'What is he thinking of?', he exclaimed. "Clean out the old leaven, separate yourselves from evil?" Are we to drop out? All keep our mouths shut? See to the holy society and turn our backs on the wicked world?'

'Didn't I always say that you take your worldly affairs too lightly?' Melas told him, suddenly and amazingly on your side.

The dispute was in full swing, and the differences over our faith, so far only simmering, boiled over: flight from the world against involvement in the world, a committed way of life against a demonstration of freedom, discipline against faith. The 'strong'

22

called the anxious 'weaklings', and they retorted by saying that the others were showing off in the faith; people accused one another of a lack of conscience or a cult of the conscience, idolatry on one side, fanatical purity on the other. There were accusations, sharp remarks, shouting, tears. And all we wanted to do was to celebrate the festival.

Timothy wasn't in an easy position. He was attacked, asked to take sides: 'What do you think?' Clearly he had to take your side, to answer for you, but at the same time he began to sense what some people had hitherto only thought quietly to themselves: 'Why doesn't the apostle come? He sends representatives: first Apollos, then Titus and now Timothy – but no Paul.' Really, you should have been there, not a substitute. What could we discuss with Timothy? He wasn't prepared for the onslaught. And more and more views kept being expressed, getting more and more confusing. Question after question, standpoints, doubts about other people's faith.

The man who had been the cause of this had long since disappeared. He had taken advantage of the arguing to slip away. No one gave him a thought.

Finally Timothy suggested that that very night we should compose a letter to you and give this task to a working party. The majority agreed, and people got very interested. Twelve of us, including me and Timothy, met after the meal in Gaius' study: Quartus and Boaz were there, Melas and Chrysallis, Phalakros and Oknos, Mara and Xenia, Gaius the householder and Krispos, who was the spokesman. Timothy had asked him to be the leader, probably because he thought that an older brother would do this better than he could, and because he assumed that the old synagogue president would have had practice in this.

[Of those mentioned I still have to introduce Phalakros and Oknos to you. Phalakros you must know: a bald-headed young man; he used to earn his living as a male prostitute – do you remember? Now he lives on casual work. Oknos is a friend of his: a freeman from Sicily; he works as a cook in a restaurant in the square by the theatre. The rest you'll already know.]

The working party was big enough for the different standpoints to be represented properly. Not completely:[38] there were no slaves – the port workers, all those who have to be at work before dawn and also have a long journey home. We had celebrated the supper at first cock-crow,[39] and then they had to leave. Only Mara, who doesn't have to be at her pub until noon, insisted on being there. The others had gone. A pity, since we also talked about the situation of slaves. You'll read it. Otherwise tonight's work has been almost intolerable for me. I too have to be in the office on time tomorrow morning, unlike a brother like Boaz or a sister like Xenia. But not before daybreak, like the others. I won't complain. A fair copy of the letter has now been written out, and Quartus is taking it to the port tomorrow on his first trip to Kenchreai.

Greetings to you from Tertius, the secretary.

Christ is risen! The power of the Lord be with you!

The church in Corinth, Achaia

to

Paul, the apostle, now in Ephesus, Asia

God's friendship be with you and remain with you!
We greet you with the song we sang this passover night, which Esther sang for us:

> Christ is free,
> none can compel him.
> All things are his,
> heaven and earth,
> present and future,
> angels and powers,
> life and light.

> Christ is free:
> none can compel us.
> We are Christ's,
> Paul is ours,
> Cephas, Apollos,
> all are ours,
> for we are Christ's.

We were glad to get your letter, dear brother Paul. You've shown us the gospel of Jesus, and that has given us new life. We're also very ready to take your critical comments to heart. But some questions have arisen among us over which we differ. We want to put them to you. At the end of your letter you asked us to clear the decks, to clean out the old leaven and rigorously break off contacts with adulterers, idolaters and other godless people. At any rate, that's what some people thought to be the gist of what you were saying at the end. Those among us who've always practised and called for a clear break with the world saw what you said as confirmation of their views. They're afraid of God's saints being soiled by contact with the pollution of the world and its idols. So for example they avoid even touching meat which has been used in sacrifices to idols. Some don't eat meat at all, even when it's offered them by friends, and others make sure when buying meat that it doesn't come from some sacrificial altar. We Jews have always been accustomed to seeing that our food is clean, and for some of us even now, anything unclean is an abomination.'

Thus Krispos. Now Boaz:

'Yes, and we'll keep on doing this; we won't be talked out of it by any Greek, not even a Greek brother. You've got to understand that this isn't some little quirk of us Jews. It would make us just like Greeks, and we've got to be firm. Let me tell you about my son, for example. Jonah has just turned seventeen, and he's already been shown what it means to say a firm no here, to keep refusing when the boys invite him to a party where there's heaps of meat. He has to put up with the mockery and the teasing, when he explains why not. Recently they turned up at our place one night, stuffed full of food, roaring drunk and shouting their heads off, and tipped the gnawed remains of their feasting through Jonah's window. And the Greeks say that meat is unimportant!'

'Not all Greeks,' Chrysallis interrupts. 'Many of us think and live just as you do. For example, Melas never eats meat; Rufina, Timon and many others avoid all contact with sacrifices. It's no longer our world. We've gone through the water, we're steeped in the spirit, and we've left that kind of thing behind us. All flesh. The flesh of the cults of idols and the flesh of the sexes. I agree with you, Paul, we're "pure dough" for the Lord's passover; our souls are temples of the divine spirit;[40] we've turned our back on all flesh and its lusts. You're right. Everyone should do this! All the true saints!'

Quartus can hardly contain himself:

'What am I to say to this, dear Paul? Above all, what am I to do? You remember: three years ago, when you went off to Ephesus, I'd just begun my transport business. I've built it up, but it's taken me all my energy. Now I've eight teams going between the harbours and a couple of donkeys; I employ fifteen people, including the cowgirls, and at last I've been able to marry. My wife is pregnant with our third child. And now: am I to leave them all in the lurch? My people, my children? My wife? You may remember that no transport business on the Isthmus has a chance without the great Babbios.[41] He controls everything that moves or carries things between Lechaion and Kenchreai.[42] This rich and flashy dandy sets himself up as a patron. Now, for example, he's celebrating the betrothal of his daughter to the son of a shipowner (and with it his move into the shipping world). He has a tremendous party, and everyone has to go: all "his" drovers, coachmen, loaders, baggage-carriers and donkey-drivers, all are invited. It's an expression of his generosity. We have to make a pilgrimage out to his country house, spend a whole night there, live it up, all be buddies. Of course there's masses of meat and clearly it's come from the altars. For there are plenty of sacrifices to the gods. Our noble Babbios regards himself as a favourite of the gods. And of course there are plenty of whores, not to mention boys. No one can afford to turn Babbios down. I once belonged to him. He bought me as a child almost thirty years ago. Evidently I was too keen and too well brought up; anyway, as one of his whims he was generous enough to free me. I've obligations to him. I must do him the honours, a compliment here, a gesture there; it all helps one get on. It's no use. All freemen have to do this.[43] Like a slave you have to obey, and that's that. Now I have my transport business and I want to keep it. I can't say, "Dear Babbios, I owe you my freedom, your parties make me feel sick, and the meat that you serve is an abomination." Old Babbios himself is a freeman; as a young lad he was the property of a noble Roman family.

That's what I want to get across to those who aim to build a church simply of free men and women here. Think hard! We all long for freedom. And soon it will come in the kingdom of God. Then we shall finally be free. But not before that, I assure you.

But tell me, Paul, what am I to do? I've a family, two small children and a third on the way. How am I to look after them? If I were single, it would be fine. But as things are? Should I give up the business? Work somewhere as a cellarman or a builder? I'll do it, for Christ's sake, I'll do it if you say, "That's the way". But as long as I'm not sure that it has to be that way, I'll go on working and also butter up Babbius, let him serve me meat, sing his praises and think my own thoughts.'

'It would have been best if you hadn't taken a wife,' Melas now interjects. 'It's best anyway for a man not to touch a woman.[44] You're a particularly striking example of what that can lead to.'

'Just shut up, Melas!' Phalakros has sprung to his feet and has put a protective hand on Quartus' shoulder. 'Why are you giving him a lousy conscience? Has that anything to do with the faith in Christ that you preach?'

'I'm quite ready to show you how continence and faith go together.' Melas starts another lecture, but Krispos tips Phalakros the wink and lets him speak first.

'We know all about this,' he declares. 'We're reasonable people. Idols aren't real. We have one God, and all the others exist only in the minds of the unredeemed, and their power is nothing but imagination. This society which builds its altars and its temples is played out; at any rate it's become insignificant for us believers. There's nothing more that can harm us: what can pieces of meat which have been dedicated to some figment of the imagination do to us? Why are Melas, Chrysallis and their like asking us to be above worldly things which have long lost their substance? You've confirmed it yourself, Paul: everything belongs to us. Everything! Nothing is untouchable any longer, nothing is tabu. Why should we go by the consciences of the insecure, who still haven't understood?' He turns to Melas: 'The freedom to eat and drink also has to do with faith. You must have found that at some point. There you are, sitting in the midst of a horde of idolaters, eating their meat and drinking wine with them; you feel their holy dread and their anxious concern not to cause the gods any trouble – and it doesn't affect you at all. Something that only a few years ago would have made you tremble, would have taken your breath away, is finished. You know all about this! You have knowledge! I can tell you, that builds you up. You're free! You can do anything. What can eating meat from a sacrifice or touching a woman do to you?'

Now Melas speaks again. Unmoved, he looks Phalakros in the eye. 'I can agree on one thing. Everything earthly is insignificant. The world with it goings-on and this dirty, smelly body[45] and its urges. What the blinkered see as the work of idols is in fact nothing but insubstantial delusion. But once we've recognized this, can we go on as though we were of this world? I say no. You know, Paul, with all due respect, that I owe my knowledge and insight to Apollos. Nevertheless, you were always an example for me in one thing: you didn't touch a woman. The body with its desires has succumbed to the world of nothingness. The meat on the altars serves the delusions of vain idols. Anyone who has knowledge abhors delusions. Yes, clean out the old leaven. Clean out anything that claims to be essential!'

'Moreover,' says Boaz, pushing forward, 'an apostle passing through Corinth once told me that when you were in Jerusalem you entered into a commitment to forbid all churches to eat meat offered to idols or to fornicate with women.'[46]

Timothy shakes his head in amazement at this remark. He's never heard anything of the sort, he declares, either from Paul or from Titus.

'Look,' Gaius remarks, 'your argument rests on very weak premises. It sounds conclusive and consistent, but how does it work out in practice? Every time you're asked out, are you going to interrogate your hostess painstakingly before eating her roast? How are you going to live, here in Corinth, without coming into contact with all the inessentials? Wherever you go, you bump into idolatry. The shopping centre is full of idols and altars. You get water from consecrated springs. Every banqueting hall is attached to a sanctuary. If you have to go into the city offices you've got to pass between statues of gods. So what? We know that they aren't anything. So don't impose any unnecessary scruples on people. Think about the poor among us: where are they to eat their fill, if you forbid them to go to the public festivals with their portions of meat?'[47]

'Moreover,' Quartus butts in, 'how are we to make friends if we put up the shutters? None of the twenty-six whom we baptized yesterday would have found their way to the faith if we'd anxiously avoided contact with them.'

Finally it's Oknos' turn. He would rather have had his say straight after Phalakros, but Krispos had asked him to be patient. 'I'm with Phalakros,' Oknos declares, 'and many of us think in just the same way. Meat isn't important. It's not something for believers to worry about. We can do anything. Freedom is what builds us up. Food for the belly and the belly for food, isn't that it? So don't get me arguing with Christ.'

Mara flares up. 'Have we sunk so low as to take as our guide a bawdy old song that the drunkards shout out in the pubs? Do you know how this ditty goes on, Oknos? Or don't they sing such hits in your noble theatre tavern? I'll sing it for you, since poor Oknos doesn't dare to. You ought to hear what I have to listen to, night after night, blaring in my ears.' And she rolls her eyes like a drunkard and grinds out in a screeching voice:

Food for the belly,
the belly for food.
Have a nice day,
till they decay,
belly and food.

Bodies for women,
and women for bodies.
Try the 'Come hither',
till you both wither,
bodies and women.

Let's eat our fill,
drink all we will,
take what's on offer,
food, wine and bed,
tomorrow we're dead.

Don't be cross with me, Paul, for letting you in for such disgusting stuff. I suspect that some brothers talk in such a starchy way only so that they can quietly enjoy themselves with the prostitutes.[48] That's why they put on airs and bruise the consciences of the insecure.'

'It's a crude song,' says Gaius, 'but it does have a point. Everything belongs to us. We can do anything. It doesn't harm our relationship with God. I think that's what Onkos meant. So let's leave the pub hit aside. Let's talk about the freedom we have in Christ. For example, Fulvia has been a widow for two years now, and is longing for a husband. As far as I know, she wants to marry again when she gets better. Some people in the church think that's not on. Widows remain widows, they say. So where's the freedom of Christ?'

'You're only taking Fulvia's side because you want a new wife yourself,' says Melas darkly.

'No,' Gaius retorts, 'I'm still mourning the death of my wife too deeply. Though in the long run you may be right. But be that as it may, I won't let you dictate to me whether I should get married later or remain single.'

'I want to say something else to our young people.' Krispos himself begins to speak. 'They're in love and they're very insecure. People tell them that it's a sin if they want one another and are longing to marry. Some of them rightly feel pressurized by such a principle, that it's best not to touch a woman at all.'

'I really don't understand you, brothers and sisters,' retorts Chrysallis. 'I don't want to dictate anything to you. I'm neither your apostle or your teacher. But I belong to Christ, and Christ belongs to you. I don't want to be some man's property any more. I find it strange that someone who has received Christ in her soul can give her body to a man. It seems strange to me that any of us can go on thinking of anything like marriage. I can't. I don't need to marry. I've everything with which to live a full life in Christ. I give myself to him in prayer, I sink into him to become one with him and see his glory. What more do I need?'

'But you also know,' retorts Krispos, 'how much my grand-daughter Hannah, who is fourteen, is impressed by you, and how she worships you as her model of deep faith. Yet at the same time she loves young Fortunatus, Stephanas' nephew, and of course the two of them are passionately longing to become one.[49] Poor Hannah is torn this way and that, and she's already thinking of having a "spiritual" marriage like Esther and Mattat, in which only their souls unite and not their bodies.[50] But how can that work with two people who're so young? Please, Paul, do clear things up for us; tell us what the Lord wants of us.'

'How do you know that Esther and Mattat are living a continent life?' Phalakros interrupts. 'Only because they don't have any children. No one knows, and no one has asked them. Or have you?'

'No,' says Krispos, 'but some fanatics in the church talk about them as though their continence were the only right life-style. Some who are insecure are keeping away from their wives as a precaution, as though they had leprosy, and some wives are driving their husbands out of their double bed, as though they were utterly indecent in wanting to make love. That's what the talk about Mattat and Esther is leading to.'

'It doesn't much matter whether Mattat and Esther are living together continently or not,' Melas lectures us. 'The only important question is whether freedom in the spirit is compatible with a physical bond to another human being. If not, then that applies to all of us, and not just to Esther and Mattat.'

Xenia, so agitated that she's going red in the face, reminds Krispos that she had indicated that she wanted to speak a long time before. Now that she can have her say she shrieks at Melas – as much as a lady of a better class can shriek at anyone. 'Do you want to split our families and break up marriages? Sow discord and incite people to get divorced? Do you holy solitaries know what keeping a family together involves? Do you know about getting on with a husband who is extremely suspicious about our cause?'

Boaz chips in: 'The family's important to me, dear Xenia, but in your case there's another issue. You have a Gentile partner. Or has your husband recently applied for baptism, to wash himself clean of his godlessness? I've not seen him. Members of the family who are unbelievers are as intolerable to us as meat on the altars of idols.[51] Intercourse with a Gentile pollutes you. It makes the whole church unclean. But the church is holy. There's only one thing for it, divorce! Away with the old leaven!'

'So,' hisses Xenia, finding it difficult to keep control of herself, 'you've just called my husband old leaven, dirty, and I'm to clear him out. And with him Leah's partner, and Erastos' wife and many others who are lovingly partnered with one or other of us. Let's see whether Paul meant that. And let's look at the scriptures, to discover whether God thinks like that about the love of two people. So Paul, write to us soon! I expect an answer from you which is guided by the spirit of God and not by abstruse ideas.'

Krispos, anxious to calm things down and get to the end, sums up: 'You see, brother Paul, there are different standpoints; it's difficult to be of the same opinion and for all of us to pull in the same direction, as you rightly tell us to. We're urgently waiting for your instructions. Surely you can sort out all these disputed questions in a direction we can all take?'

'But that needn't mean that the same thing always applies to everyone,' Boaz prolongs the discussion once again. 'There are some who want to take equality among us to extremes, not only in church but also in public. They say that if there is neither slave nor free in the community of Christ, no one should be a slave any more, and that the rich among us should buy the freedom of all the brothers and sisters who are not free as soon as possible. I say that these are utopian dreams. Quartus has rightly warned us against them.'

Gaius also has something to contribute on this question. 'I'm of two minds here. As I understand the gospel, we should really all be free. From now on no brother or sister should belong to any other master than Christ. That's why I also freed Chrysallis when she joined the church: she still goes on working with me, of her own free will, and I pay her. But this raised false hopes among others in the business. Some came to our gatherings in the expectation that they would then be freed, and found Leah telling them to their faces, with her prophetic acuteness, that they were wanting to do a deal with God. That offended some of them. It's more difficult in practice than I first expected.'

'Who can think up such crazy things?', exclaims Boaz, shaking his head. 'As if there could be only free people in the world! In the end they'll want men to go around like women or women like men, or we Jews like the uncircumcised. They'll send us to the surgeon to have a new foreskin fitted, like those vain sportsmen who're ashamed of their Jewish origins. My son Jonah could tell you stories about his friends.'[52]

'No one will drag you to the surgeon, Boaz,' says Mara, 'but that doesn't mean that everything has to stay the same. What do you have against the dream that differences of status could disappear – not only here among us, but also around us in the city? All over the province? All round the islands? All over the world? Why shouldn't women live like men and slaves like free people? Everywhere? Why should we keep this experience to ourselves, as if it were stolen treasure?'

Boaz retorts: 'Because it's nonsense, other-worldly nonsense, and we simply make fools of ourselves with it.'

And Mara, 'Just think. It's twenty-five years since the Lord's resurrection. Since then people have been waiting for him to come. We also waited for him this passover night, but so far he hasn't come. So we can count on another twenty-five years . . .' General laughter. Another twenty-five years! No one can really imagine that. 'All right, let's say ten years. Ten years for this world. We're something like the head office of God's universal society. We're the model for a new humanity, redeemed from being split up into the free, the freed and the slaves; into Jews, Greeks and foreigners; into men, women and children. The world could be transformed if it followed our example.'

'Too much respect for a world which is passing away,' says Melas, and Krispos finds it difficult to bring the excitement under control. He wants to finish the letter off, but Oknos stops him once again.

'Just one more thing,' says Oknos, the cook: 'Listen, Paul: you can't have intended Titius Justus to treat me as he did. Let me point out that at the time I was an unsuspecting unbeliever. Things were going badly with me. No work, no food. I had to borrow money. Titus lent me sixty drachmas. I couldn't pay it back. I went into his shoemaker's workshop and asked for a postponement. He said. "You've got it; in the kingdom of God that kind of thing doesn't count. There are no poor and rich here" – or something like that. Before witnesses. There were two customers – I can name them – and a friend of mine. Now that I'm a member of the church he wants it back again. He's asking for it back with interest.[53] Titius the just![54] Is that the way for brothers to treat one another? Don't people need to keep promises they made outside any longer? What do you think, Paul?'

All patience is exhausted. And at the same time everyone is agreed on one thing. These quarrels don't belong here. 'You've got a date in court,' scolds Quartus, 'let your trivialities be decided there and spare us. Any pagan judge will have enough sense to see how you're mixing up religion and business here.'

And Krispos says soothingly: 'Yes, dear Oknos, we really aren't responsible for such things now.' He takes the opportunity of really getting to the end: 'Dear brother Paul, you see how sometimes one opinion clashes with another here. Perhaps even as you read this letter you can feel how individuals are putting forward your convictions with all their hearts. We long for you to clarify things. You gave us hope with your promise to come soon. And we want to do all we can to see that you don't come among us with a whip but with love and a tender spirit. However, since presumably you won't be setting out as early as next week, do write soon. You must excuse us if we sometimes doubt whether we shall ever see you again. We've been separated from you too long.

At any rate, we're grateful to you for sending Timothy. He sends his greetings. He expects to spend another two weeks in Corinth, and then he wants to look round the churches in the province, and after that make another stop with us. We shall equip him for the journey back.

You wrote to us about the hostility that you're suffering in Ephesus, and Timothy has also told us something about it. That's shaken us. We can hardly imagine what you're going through there. We're praying daily for you, your colleagues and all the brothers and sisters in Asia. May God protect you and bring your troubles ot an end.

Timothy, your friend and colleague, and Gaius, our host, greet you in love. And all those who have written this letter send their greetings: Quartus and Boaz, Melas and Chrysallis, Phalakros and Oknos, Mara and Xenia, Krispos, your brother, and Tertius, who has taken the notes. All the saints from Corinth greet you.

Peace be with you.

It's also worth mentioning something else. When everyone had gone and I, too, was about to leave, I saw Chrysallis sitting all by herself in the half-light of the dawning day, bent over your letter, spelling out the same passage again and again. 'He quoted my song,' she muttered. 'What has he done with it? Has he spoilt it? Turned it upside down? Or joined in in a new key?'

Paul and Sosthenes, our brother and yours

to

the church of God in Corinth

Grace be to you and peace from God our Father and the Lord Jesus Christ.

I thank my God daily for all of you, that you're making the gospel known to many, and devoting yourselves to it with undiminished passion, so that you're growing more and more, and God is bringing you men and women from all over the world. I trust that God will also make the knowledge of his will grow in you, so that you increase in understanding – for the gospel and for one another. That's why I'm also glad, brothers and sisters, that you decided to write to me again immediately. In this way I can correct your misunderstandings.[55]

I wrote to you in my letter not to have any contact with adulterers. Of course I don't mean the adulterers of this world or the greedy and robbers and idolaters generally – in that case you would indeed have to drop out of the world! Rather, I wrote to you that you should break off contact with anyone who calls himself a brother if he is an adulterer, greedy, an idolater, a blasphemer, a drunkard or a robber. You aren't even to eat with such a person. As for judging outsiders – what concern of mine is that? Those inside the church are the ones you're to judge. God will judge those outside. So drive out the wicked from your midst!

Now, about lawsuits.[56] Is one of you in fact ready to go to law with another before a pagan court instead of before the saints? Don't you know that the saints will judge the world? And if the world is to be judged by you, aren't you responsible for trying trivial cases? Don't you know that we shall even be judges over the angels? So why not over everyday problems? All right, you have disputes over trivia: but why do you bring them in particular before judges who count for nothing in the church? I tell you, it's shameful. Is there really no one among you, no one wise enough to arbitrate between two brothers? No, one brother goes to law against another, and before unbelievers at that.

It's already a lapse to have lawsuits against each other at all. Why don't you prefer to suffer wrong? Why don't you prefer to lose something? But on the contrary, you add more injustice, you take away what belongs to others – and brothers at that. Don't you know that people who wrong others won't inherit the kingdom of God? Don't deceive yourselves:

> Prostitutes and idolaters,
> adulterers and rent boys,
> perverts, thieves and the greedy,
> drunkards, blasphemers and robbers,
> will not inherit the kingdom of God.[57]

Some of you were like that. But you've been washed, sanctified, put right by the name of the Lord Jesus Christ and the Spirit of our God.

'I can do anything' – yes. But not everything helps. 'I can do anything' – but I don't want to become dependent on anything.

'Food for the belly, the belly for food.' God will destroy belly and food. The body isn't meant for going to prostitutes; it's meant for the Lord, and the Lord for the body: God has raised the Lord, and he will similarly raise us by his power. You know that your bodies are members of Christ. So can I take the members of Christ and make them members of a prostitute? That can't be right. Don't you know that someone who joins himself to a prostitute is one body with her? For – as scripture says –

> 'the two shall become one flesh'.

But anyone who is joined to the Lord is one Spirit with him. Keep away from prostitution. Look, every mistake that a person makes happens outside the body. But anyone who has dealings with prostitutes sins against his own body, against himself. Have you forgotten that your body is a house of the Holy Spirit, which you have from God? God dwells in you. You don't belong to yourselves: for you have been freed, and the price has been paid. So honour God with your body!

Now for the things you wrote about: 'Wouldn't it be best anyway for a man not to touch a woman? My view is that, rather than going to prostitutes, it's better for each man to have his own wife and each wife her husband. The husband should give his wife her due, and the wife the husband his due. For the wife's body isn't hers to dispose of, but her husband's; and the husband's body isn't his to dispose of, but his wife's. Don't refuse one another, except at most by agreement for a short time, in order to find restfulness for prayer, and then come together again, so that Satan doesn't tempt you with uncontrollable desires. Here I'm just making suggestions, not laying down the law. What I would like best would be for everyone to be without ties, like me. But each has their own special gift before God: one this, and one that.

So I'm telling the unmarried and the widowed that it's good for them to remain as I am. But if they can't live a continent life, they should marry. It's better to marry than to burn with desire.

My instructions for the married, or rather, not mine, since the Lord has given this instruction, is that the wife shouldn't separate from her husband – and if she's already separated from him, she should remain unmarried or be reconciled to her husband – and that the husband shouldn't divorce his wife.

Otherwise, *I* say, and not the Lord: if a brother has a wife who is an unbeliever and she agrees to live with him, he shouldn't divorce her. And a woman with an unbelieving husband who agrees to live with her shouldn't divorce her husband. For the unbelieving husband is made holy by the wife, and the unbelieving wife is made holy by the brother. If that weren't the case, your children would be unclean, but as it is, they are holy. But if the unbelieving partner wants to separate, he or she should separate. In such a case the brother or the sister isn't bound slavishly. God has called you to freedom. Wife, do you know whether your husband will be saved? Or husband, do you know whether your wife will be saved?

However, everyone should keep to the kind of life which the Lord has assigned him, the one which he had when God called him. This is also my ruling for all the churches. If anyone was called when circumcised, he shouldn't have an artificial foreskin!

And if anyone was called when not circumcised – he shouldn't be circumcised now. For circumcision is nothing and the foreskin is nothing; what matters is keeping God's commandments. You should all remain quietly in the state in which you were called. If you were a slave when you were called – don't let that bother you! And even if you can get your freedom – prefer to remain a slave![58] For the slave who was called by the Lord is a freeman of the Lord's. Similarly, the freeman who is called is a slave of Christ's. You've been freed; the price has been paid. You needn't become slaves of men. Before God, brothers and sisters, everyone can remain as they were when they were called.

I have no rule from the Lord for young people, but I can give you my opinion: through the mercy of the Lord I'm trustworthy enough. I think that in view of the impending catastrophes it would be good, that is, it would be good for a man to remain as he is. If you're attached to a young woman, then don't try to separate. If you're living without a woman, then don't look for one. But even if you marry, it's not a sin. And if a girl marries, of course she isn't sinning either. But such young people will have to undergo all kinds of painful experiences, and I would prefer to spare you that. For I say to you, brothers and sisters,

> The times are closing in,
> in future it must be that
> those who have wives live as though they had none,
> those who weep as though there were nothing to weep for,
> those who rejoice as though there were no joy,
> those who buy as though they couldn't keep anything,
> and those who have dealings with the world
> as though they had nothing to do with it.
> For the fabric of this world is falling apart.[59]

I want you to be able to be free from anxiety. Someone who is single can be completely devoted to the things of the Lord, can seek to please the Lord. But those who are married must also think about pleasing their wives, and so they're divided. The single woman or girl can also devote herself wholly to the things of the Lord, so as to be holy in body and soul. The married woman has to bother about worldly things, and think how to please her husband. I'm telling you this for your benefit, not to pressurize you, but so that you can be bound to the Lord respectably and over a long period, without other things getting in the way. But if anyone thinks that it's not fair on his girl-friend, where sexual passions are over-ripe,[60] if it's necessary, let him do what he desires. He won't sin. They should marry. But if anyone has made up his mind of his own free will, under no pressure, has his own desires under control,[61] and has decided of his own free will not to touch his girl-friend – good for him. So it's fine to marry a girl-friend, but even better not to.[62]

A wife is bound to her husband as long as he lives. If her husband dies, she's free to marry whoever she likes. However, she should do so in the Lord. But in my view she'll be happier if she remains unmarried, and I think that I too have the spirit of God.

On the question of sacrificing to idols. Obviously, we know all about this. Being a know-all puffs you up; love builds you up. Anyone who imagines that he's grasped something is far from having grasped as he needs to grasp. But anyone who loves God is grasped by him.

So, on eating meat offered to idols: we all know that in reality there are no idols, and that there is no God but one. And even if so-called gods in heaven and on earth lead people astray – and there are indeed masses of gods and lords – we have

one God,
the Father,
from whom are all things
and for whom we exist,
and one Lord, Jesus Christ,
through whom all things exist
and we through him.

However, not everyone has this knowledge. For some people the idols whom they have served up till now are still too near, and when they eat meat, for them it's like sacrificing to an idol. Because their conscience is insecure, it's troubled. Certainly eating doesn't bring down God's judgment on us. We lose nothing if we don't eat, and we gain nothing if we do. But make sure that your sovereign freedom doesn't become a problem for the insecure. For if someone sees you sitting at a table in the temple of idols, in full possession of your knowledge, won't that encourage him, insecure though he is in his conscience, to eat meat offered to idols? In that case this insecure person may be destroyed by your knowledge, this brother for whom Christ died! If you offend in this way against the brothers and sisters, and wound their insecure consciences, you're offending against Christ himself. So if food is hell for my brother, I would prefer never to eat meat again, so as not to cause my brother hell.

[The dictation is interrupted and the letter continues after the arrival of the following letter from Corinth – on p.50.]

Stephanas, church member in Corinth, and Fortunatus and Achaikos

to

Paul the apostle of Christ, in Ephesus, Province of Asia

May the goodness of Christ be with you and the truth of our God shine on you!
I'm sending you this letter in haste, dear brother Paul, barely three days after the previous one went off to you, since something has happened that you must know about as soon as possible.

Yesterday afternoon my nephew Fortunatus arrived with two travellers. They had come up from Kenchreai, asked him about work in the vineyards and wanted directions to my house. They explained that they were brothers from a church in Syria,[63] travelling through, and were curious to learn more about the church in Corinth. They said that people were talking about it all over the world, and about Paul, its founder. They showed me a letter from the church which had sent them and pointed to the seal as confirmation of their commission.

I told them that they had come at a good time, because some brothers and sisters would certainly be meeting that evening, and that Timothy would also be there. I said that when they had had refreshed themselves, I would go with them into the city to Gaius' villa. No, they said, there was time enough for that; their most important destination was the house of Stephanas, in other words my house, since they had been told that I was a reliable witness to events. So I showed them to a room and waited for them with the table laid.

'As we told you, dear brother,' they began the proceedings – for in fact this conversation soon seemed to me more like the interrogation of a witness than a friendly exchange between brothers – 'as we told you, we've heard a lot about you and your house; that the first church met here, outside the gates of the city, that you and your family were the first to respond to the gospel, and that you've therefore been witness from the start to the actions of those who have been at work here. You're a reliable man who loves the truth, and everyone trusts you to give a sound, balanced judgment.'

I asked them in amazement who had brought such news about us to Syria. They referred to the many apostles and preachers travelling through, who on their way up and down the world kept going through Corinth, since all the routes pass through the Isthmus, from north to south and from east to west. These itinerant preachers had always spoken of Stephanas with great respect. However, they had also reported things – not only from Corinth but from the whole area of Achaia, Macedonia, Asia and Cyprus, in fact from all the churches for which Paul and Barnabas felt responsible. As they said, people had heard things which made them prick up their ears and which needed to be looked into, so as not to do anyone an injustice. They had been chosen to make enquiries, and I was the right person to help them to discover the truth.

I wanted to know what kind of rumours were going the rounds which led them to travel around at such expense, interrogating brothers and sisters, and who was so keen to bring the truth to light.

They both laughed knowingly and gave me a little lecture on events of recent times: 'The difficulties began with the summit meeting in Jerusalem,'[64] they explained. 'That was seven years ago. This was an attempt to clarify at the highest level under what conditions the gospel was to be spread among Jews and Gentiles. Antioch had become the centre of the mission to the Gentiles. Paul and Barnabas were working from there, in other words as part of the team from this action centre, on behalf of the church of Antioch. At the time they were real "apostles", i.e. "delegates", authorized representatives of the church.[65] They also went to the negotiations in Jerusalem as "delegates". It was a summit meeting between the "apostles" of two centres: on the one hand James, John and Cephas for Jerusalem and the Jewish churches, and on the other Barnabas and Paul from Antioch and the churches made up of both Jews and non-Jews. You will have heard how after vigorous arguments[66] both parties managed to struggle to an agreement which all could seal with a handshake. That's how people tell it everywhere, and it's true. However, the result – presented cautiously – needed to be interpreted. That soon became evident. At any rate, Paul and Barnabas interpreted it as though they hadn't incurred any obligations.'[67]

'Wait a minute,' I corrected them, 'what about the financial support for the brothers and sisters in Jerusalem?' I told them that this commitment had always been extremely important to you.

'The collection, certainly,' he conceded, 'we'll come back to that. But otherwise they used the agreement as *carte blanche* to allow just about anything in their churches and to pay no heed to the Jewish brothers. Further negotiations were needed. James, the brother of the Lord, had already circulated proposals about the points on which the Gentile brothers should accommodate the Jews. Cephas attempted to act as mediator, visited the church at Antioch, overcame his abhorrence of the uncircumcised and sat down at table with them; however, he didn't want to unsettle the delegates from James and endanger a compromise which was within reach – at all events, it was Paul and Barnabas who stubbornly and immovably insisted on their interpretation of the Jerusalem agreement.'

I interrupted them. I said that I'd been told that Barnabas was ready for compromise and would have preferred to follow Cephas' line, but his vacillating made you, Paul, so angry that after that you didn't want to work with him any more. That's right, isn't it, or am I mistaken?

'We should have known that you weren't properly informed about this undesirable development,' the brothers complimented me. 'You're quite right: Paul even split with Barnabas at that time. You can see how incapable this man is of respecting a colleague who moves even a finger's breadth from his own position.'

I now protested energetically about these insinuations and emphasized that the brothers were supposed to have come to hear the truth from me. If they wanted to hear the truth about Paul, I could tell them many good things.

'Excuse us,' said one of them, who so far had simply nodded his head in confirmation. 'sometimes my brother's zeal gets the better of his good judgment. In fact we're no longer concerned about the old stories but about the present. We still need to clear up the question who is spreading the message of Christ properly in a church which has now become worldwide, and who is justified in presenting himself as an apostle. And we see a break in the careers of both Paul and Barnabas: immediately after the unpleasant arguments in Antioch, both set off on their own initiative, and no longer as delegates of the church of Antioch. They may have done good work, but they did it for themselves, and not as delegates of a church that sent them. A mission is part of being an apostle, and Barnabas and Paul have no credentials for a mission. They no longer qualify for the title apostle. And that has noticeably jeopardized their work. At any rate, that's the present state of our research.'

Again I protested. 'Paul has always presented himself as an apostle of Christ. He's never claimed to be the delegate of a church. Christ himself has sent him.'

'We shall see,' the first of the two remarked again, 'whether this claim holds up. That's why we're carrying out this investigation. Clarity is vital. Do you know what some people are already saying about Paul? They nickname him "the freak". Born too late, a deformed apostle, hardly viable. Of course we're concerned to stop such mockery once and for all. It damages the whole church of Christ if jokes like that can be made about leading figures. Unfortunately – you won't like it, but I have to say it – unfortunately Paul himself doesn't feel convinced about his own mission.'

I felt this conversation getting weirder and weirder. What would they bring up next? What kind of suspicions would they sow among the brothers and sisters? In my mind I thanked God that they'd come to me first. I saw in my mind's eye the insecure faces of some brothers and sisters whose faith would begin to crumble if such doubts were cast on 'their' apostle. How could I spare them that? Quietly, my eyes fixed on the two visitors, I prayed to Christ for clear understanding and wisdom.

'What do you mean by that?' I asked. 'Give me some facts!'

'He doesn't behave like an apostle,' they explained. 'He doesn't exercise the rights that he would have as an apostle, which are guaranteed him by Christ himself: hospitality and care. We hear that from almost all the communities. He finances his enterprise himself. No delegate acts like that. Not an apostle of the Lord. That's the behaviour of someone working on his own initiative. We suspect that the same thing is true of Barnabas; we're still waiting for the results of the investigation. Some of the brothers are on his track in Cyprus. Questions are being raised there. Some get answered, some don't. For example, why does a man finance his own missionary activity? Beause he's well aware that he has no right to claim support like an apostle. In that case, why does he work as though he were one? Does he want to gain influence and honour, or even more? What moves him to curry favour with the Greeks and their modernistic thought? How can he uncritically adapt to the Western life-style? He won't ask for anything, won't impose on others. All things to all men.[68] He bestows the grace of God and even pays his own expenses. What drives him to do that? Where does he get the money from? It's said that he works, sews tents. Is what he earns by doing that enough? He's said to live modestly. But what about the travelling? Isn't that expensive? And does he always get work immediately in places where he makes a new beginning? You see, brother Stephanas, one question leads to another. And somewhere along the line we come across the collection of money for the saints in Jerusalem. And the zeal with which the man asks for gifts. You confirmed this earlier. Unanswered questions, so far. We're looking for the answers.'

'I pray to God that you discover the truth,' I said. 'Not truth by human standards, but the truth which the spirit of Christ discloses.'

'That's precisely why we've come to you,' they retorted. 'You can help us and the truth. Tell us how things began here in Corinth. How Paul worked during the eighteen months he spent here, and how he lived.'

44

But I brought the conversation to an end for the moment. I said that they were my guests and that we would find another opportunity for me to tell them. Then I excused myself, gave instructions for them both to be served a good meal, asked Fortunatus to look after them carefully and went down into the city, to Gaius, in the hope of meeting some of the brothers and sisters there.

In fact a small group had gathered, but I saw that they had other worries. Rufina, Timon's wife, was sitting in the midst of them, weeping, complaining, raging, and everyone was going on at her. Since Rufina kept repeating her accusations, I soon understood what was troubling her. Timon, her husband, was being tormented by panic dreams. He often woke up in the night screaming, his whole body trembling, the bed wet with sweat. When morning finally came he felt shattered and paralysed, so that he could hardly get out of bed. She was afraid he might lose his job, since his boss wouldn't allow any shirking. He only got his position as a bookkeeper at the city finance office last autumn. Today he had dragged himself to the office and had struggled through the day; now he had collapsed on the bed, longing to sleep, and yet full of anxiety about the horrific dreams. And it was all, he complained, because Phalakros and Oknos had talked him into going with them to a sacrificial feast. Some local politicans had once again organized a public distribution of food[69] to canvass support from the people and the gods for their re-election, and the two had dragged poor Timon along with them. Since his baptism, indeed since he had decided to receive baptism, he had avoided any contact with the idol cults in which he had formerly been involved, and thus had protected the whole family from harm. He hadn't touched a piece of meat from the altars or had a sip of wine from a pagan cup. But along came the pair and persuaded him that it would build him up tremendously, and that it was a splendid feeling to eat, drink and dance at the festivities and scoff at the unsuspecting people who were offering their sacrifices to empty phantoms. Now the result of this great freedom was clear to all, and Phalakros and Oknos were to blame.

Oknos was cowering in a corner, his shoulders hunched; Phalakros was trying to play things down: 'A demon must have got hold of him, some intruder which is robbing him of his night's sleep. Get hold of Lykos, he'll drive it out.'

'We called for Lykos a long time ago, and Zinga too,' hissed Rufina, 'Lykos can't drive out a demon and Zinga can't heal him. I just don't know what to do.'

We were all at a loss. Karylla, Gaius' old housekeeper, was standing there and began to pray for Timon, as we all did. At any rate Rufina calmed down, after weeping loudly once again during the prayer. Xenia took her in her arms and promised to spend the night with her. So the two women went off.

When they'd gone, there was loud criticism of Phalakros and Oknos. 'There you have it,' Melas began, 'I can do anything! I'm allowed to do anything! Everything builds me up. Congratulations on the tremendous success of your preaching of freedom.' And some people who who hitherto hadn't joined in the argument out of uncertainty now fell on the two of them with bitter accusations. Onkos sank deeper and deeper into himself and sought protection from his friend Phalakros, who again defended himself more and more stubbornly: the connection between anxious dreams and eating at the festivities was very slim indeed; how could a believer think that insubstantial idols had so much power? Probably Timon had stomach-ache and thought that the rumblings in his stomach were demons. I felt impatient at the barren dispute. I made myself heard and said that the people who had descended on me today would have an easy time with such a divided community. And I told them about my curious guests and what they had reported.

This caused further perplexity: the insecure, who had just made their presence very much felt, fell silent, and Timotheos groaned aloud, 'It's all starting again.' He told us about similar invasions which had disturbed the Macedonian churches years earlier. That was why he'd arrived in Corinth later than Paul; he had had to turn back in Athens, to support the brothers and sisters in Thessalonike.[70]

'They mix up the truth with malicious insinuations,' remarked Leah, the midwife. 'Everyone knows that Paul earns his own living. It's no secret. But they suggest that it's a grievous crime which they must now uncover. Now Titius Justus will strike up his lament that he wasn't able to show any hospitality; Boaz and his friends will put Peter back on the pedestal; others will begin to waver, as though this church were built on quicksand, simply because its founder doesn't present any credentials for his mission, and they'll doubt the gospel because it allegedly comes from a dubious apostle. Whatever we do, the accusation will stick.'

Erastos was visibly angry, not only about the brothers from Syria, but also about you. 'Everything could have been coped with much more easily had Paul supported our investigating committee and its concern for the truth. But he was too good for it. He "saw no reason"! Critical questions have been running round the church for a long time; this afternoon isn't the first occasion on which they've arisen. Had Paul given us information at the right time, now we could deal with these intruders by giving them facts.'

Timothy said that he could give plenty of answers to the committee if that helped; after all, for six years he had been your closest colleague and a constant companion. But Leah remarked that this alone couldn't avert disaster. Timothy might be able to clear up facts and correct rumours, but both the two investigators and the insecure brothers and sisters would ask why the accused was silent about everything. 'What we need is a statement from Paul himself. It may turn his stomach, but he must defend himself now, for our sake.'

Everyone agreed with Leah. And since Tertius, our secretary, had already retired with an intolerable headache, I undertook to write all this to you. I'm doing it with my friend Achaikos, who is wielding the pen.

All this happened yesterday evening, and when I got home, ready to talk to the two brothers, they weren't there. They had gone off to walk through the city. They only came back late at night, and Achaikos, who opened the door for them, didn't ask where they'd been and whom they'd visited. So that unpleasant conversation is still to come. I wish I already had your answer!

I think a lot about you when I pray, and ask God for you to be able to continue to make Christ known with freedom and authority, despite all the troubles. All the brothers and sisters who talked with me last night send their greetings. And warmest greetings come from Fortunatus and Achaikos, my loyal colleague, who has written this letter.

The peace of God be with you!

47

Postscript

Achaikos, steward of Stephanas

to Paul

This morning I can report that the two gentlemen have got up. They've eaten: bread and milk, cheese, dried fruit and an egg. They made generous use of their right to hospitality, and not just over a meal. The staff were also at their disposal. I had to act as secretary for them: they dictated their first report on the situation immediately. Before I write out a fair copy, here's an extract.

After the heading and a few conventional greetings, they come straight to their enquiries. This is what they say:

'We have questioned some people at the home and employment of the person concerned. We were first directed to the new development on the eastern wall of the harbour, where the Jewish settlers established themselves six years ago.[71] Some people from the settlement remember how our man lived and worked there in the workshop of a certain Aquila and his wife Prisca. Aquila processed goatskins for making tents, but evidently found it very difficult to get a business going. He left again after two and a half years, presumably for Asia or even further east. The person concerned stayed with him for only a few months. Then he moved nearer the centre, right next to the synagogue, to a godfearer named Titius Justus.

We called on this man in his shoemaker's workshop. It wasn't at all easy to get anything out of him; he seemed uneasy and mistrustful. He talked a lot without saying anything, but it was clear that our man hardly ever worked in his workshop, if at all. He had money for his rent and paid for himself and his two colleagues. Titius either couldn't or wouldn't tell us where the money came from.

We asked some of the members of the church whom we met with Titius Justus about teaching and instruction, and about what principles had been handed down to them. Here there was amazing agreement. All those who had been baptized knew the most important confessions, teachings and songs for baptism, the holy meal, and the death and resurrection of the Lord. Some of the formulations were slightly different, but not the content.

However, there is a good deal of dispute in the church. We heard something about this from a certain Boaz. Our attention had been drawn to him because someone mentioned that he came from the area where Cephas was active. When asked what the points of dispute in the church were, he complained openly about certain liberal tendencies, which he opposed with all his might. However, the Jews are in a minority here. The slogans "freedom" and "equality" would confuse some people. So the church had written a letter, but was still waiting for an answer. Basically the man didn't tell us anything new, but merely confirmed what we already knew.

Finally, the collection of money for Jerusalem: they told us that this action was planned and supported by all; how it was organized still remained to be settled.

So we concentrated our further investigation on two contradictions, both connected with the way in which Paul earns his own living, of which there is clear evidence:

1. He calls himself an apostle, yet earns his own living.
2. He did hardly any work for three months, yet had enough money to support him for a year.'[72]

That's my extract from their situation report. The rest isn't important. The gentlemen will certainly use their host's staff to deliver the letter to Kenchreai. The staff will try to find a slow ship.

I'm now taking our letter straight to Erastos. It comes at a good time, since a brother from Rome has ben staying the night with him, and he's going on to Ephesus today. He'll hand over the letter to you himself. Erastos and the other brothers and sisters commend this man to you! A postman for the imperial government, he's taking express post to the provincial administration of Asia. One of the fast state boats is waiting for him. That will get him to Ephesus in three days, he says, along the direct route by the islands, if the wind is favourable.[73] Did you know that there's a church in Rome? A real church of Christ with several house churches? What Prisca and Aquila kept telling us suggested a few isolated brothers and sisters, scattered round the capital. But a genuine big church! The gospel has got there ahead of you – it's arrived in Rome before you. Get the brother to tell you about that.

49

I wish I could go with him. I'd love to see you again. Write to us soon. And God be with you!

Paul

to

the church in Corinth:

continuation[74]

Am I not free? Am I not an apostle? Haven't I seen Jesus our Lord? Aren't you my work in the Lord? If I'm not an apostle anywhere else, I am at least for you. For you are the seal on my credentials, in the Lord.

This is my defence against those who are investigating me:

Don't we have the right to eat and drink? Don't we even have the right to take with us a sister as wife, like the other apostles and the brothers of the Lord and Cephas? Or do only Barnabas and I have no right to be exempt from earning our living? Who ever serves as a mercenary at his own expense? Who plants a vineyard without eating any of its fruit? Or who looks after a herd without having some milk from it? And this isn't just a matter of common sense. Doesn't the law also say the same? It's written in the law of Moses,

'You shall not muzzle the ox when it is threshing.'

God certainly isn't so concerned about oxen. Doesn't that clearly refer to us? Indeed, for our sake he has written: whoever ploughs must be able to count on the fruit of the plough and whoever threshes must be able to count on having his share. If we've sown the seed of the Spirit in you, what is so excessive about reaping earthly fruits from you? If others claim the right from you, why shouldn't we? We haven't claimed this right at all, but we take on anything, so as not to put any obstacles in the way of the gospel of Christ.

Those who work in the sanctuary get their food from the sanctuary; those who serve the altar also serve themselves from the altar. Don't you know that? In the same way, the Lord orders that those who make the gospel known should also live by the gospel. But I haven't claimed any of this.

I'm writing this now, not so that I too should be treated in the same way. I would rather drop down dead than – no, no one will hurt my pride here! If I preach the gospel, I can't put that to my credit. For it comes over me, unavoidably, like a compulsion. If I didn't communicate it – disaster! Indeed, if I had the choice I could even get wages. But I've no choice. God has entrusted me with representing his cause. What do I get from that, then? Simply that I offer the gospel free of charge and don't exercise my right to live off the gospel.[75]

For although I'm utterly free, I've made myself the slave of all to win as many as possible. To the Jews I became a Jew to win Jews. To those under the law I became like one under the law – although I myself am not subject to the law – in order to win those who are under the law. To those outside the law I became someone outside the law – although before God I'm not outside the law, but am obligated to the law of Christ – to win the lawless. To the insecure I became insecure, to win the insecure. I've become all things to all people, to save some in any possible way.

But I do all this for love of the gospel, in order to gain a share in it. You know that all the runners in the stadium run, but only one wins the prize. So run in order to win it. A champion gives up everything else simply to win a withering garland;[76] but we win one which never withers. So I run like an athlete, who doesn't just rush anywhere, aimlessly. I fight like a boxer; I don't just flail around, but I train my body and control it, so that I don't preach to others, yet get myself disqualified

I'd like to point out to you, brothers and sisters, that our ancestors were all under the cloud and all went through the sea; they were all so to speak baptized into Moses in the cloud and in the sea. They all ate the same divine food[77] and drank the same divine drink. They drank from the divine rock which went with them. The rock was Christ.[78] Nevertheless God wasn't pleased with most of them, for they were all struck down in the wilderness.

These events have become a preview for us, so that we aren't distracted by evil, as they allowed themselves to be. So have nothing to do with the idolaters, as some of them did – as we read:

'The people sat down to eat and drink
and jumped up to dance.'

Don't let's go to prostitutes, as some of them did, and perished, twenty-thousand of them in a single day. Don't let's provoke the Lord, as some of them did, and were killed by the serpents. And don't grumble, as some of them grumbled and were destroyed by the Strangler. All this came upon them as a preview, a warning, described for us, since the end of the ages has come upon us. Therefore any of those who think they stand should take care that they don't fall.

No superhuman temptation has come upon you. And God is faithful: he won't allow you to be tempted beyond your powers, but with the temptation will create a way out, so that you can endure it.

Therefore, my dear ones, keep out of the way of the cult of idols. I'm talking to sensible people. You yourselves should judge what I say. Doesn't the cup of blessing which we bless unite us with the blood of Christ? Doesn't the bread which we break unite us with the body of Christ? Because it's *one* bread, we who are many are *one* body; for we all eat of the same bread. Look at Israel, earthly Israel: aren't all those who eat the sacrifices united with the altar?

What am I trying to say? That sacrificing to idols amounts to something? Or that an idol is something? No. But what they're offering there, they're offering to demons and not to God. You can't drink from the cup of the Lord and the cup of the demons at the same time. You can't sit at the Lord's table and the demons' table. Or are we to provoke the Lord to jealousy? Are we stronger than he is?

We can do anything, but not everything helps. We can do anything, but not everything builds us up. No one should be pursuing his or her own needs, but the needs of others.

You can eat anything sold in the market, without painstakingly investigating where it comes from. For 'the earth is the Lord's and everything in it'. If one of the unbelievers invites you to a meal and you want to accept, then eat everything that is offered without going too closely into what it is. But if some one tells you, 'this has been offered for sacrifice', then it's better not to eat it out of consideration of the person who pointed this out to you and for conscience' sake. I don't mean your own conscience, but the other person's. Why should I allow my freedom to be controlled by someone else's conscience? If I enjoy something gratefully, why should I take criticism for what I give thanks for? So whether you eat or drink, or whatever you do, do everything to the glory of God. Don't put obstacles in the way of either Jews or Greeks, or of the church of God, just as I try to please everyone in every possible way, not seeking what helps me, but what helps many people, so that they may become whole. Imitate me, as I imitate Christ.[79] And the peace of God which passes all understanding will keep watch over your thoughts and ideas in Christ Jesus.

Make sure that this letter is read out in all the house churches, and also pass it on to the church in Kenchreai.

Greet Stephanas and all his household! Also greet Quartus, the brother, with his family. Greet my colleague Timothy if he's still with you, and equip him well for the next stage of his journey.

Greet one another with the holy kiss. I greet you with my signature, *Paul*.

The grace of our Lord Jesus Christ be with you all.

Leah, Xenia and Fulvia, together with Chrysallis, Karylla, Zinga, Mara and other women of the church in Corinth

to

Paul, the apostle and brother, in Ephesus

The grace of God be with you!
We received your letter with great joy, dear Paul, and we women want to thank you for it with all our hearts. We were here in Fulvia's home, a small house church of women, since she's sick and can't get out of the house to come to the assembly. She's pretty bad; she has terrible pains and throws up everything that

she eats or drinks. We're praying with her and Zinga is laying her hands on Fulvia's forehead and her aching body. It helps for a bit, but doesn't cure her. Nevertheless, she listened to your letter from beginning to end, every word, and is intent on being here as we reply to you.

You should know that what you wrote did us good. Not just because of your impressive defence of yourself. We didn't need that at all. We're holding firm to you and aren't allowing ourselves to be put off by a couple of men passing through. But you've given many of us support in our own uncertainty. Yes, you're right: why should we listen to nonsense about what we thank God for? Some people wanted to tell us that it's a sin for women and men to love and desire one another. Fulvia was very happy and forgot her pains when she heard you say, 'You won't sin'. She thanks you and is glad for her teenage daughter; yes, and for herself too. She so longs to be with a man again, after her long period of widowhood. When she gets better.

But Chrysallis also thanks you, for herself and all those who are single like her. She's happy that you are taking her side and don't think it crazy that her longing for God means more than any earthly desire. Really to be able to live free from earthly ties is a special gift of God, as you say: 'Each has their own special gift from God, one this and one that.' Of course Chrysallis believes that by 'special gift' you meant only independence.[80] The rest of us understood you differently here: isn't it also a gift of God for two people to be able to live together in love?[81] We argued a bit about that with Chrysallis, in a very friendly way. You'll tell us, when you come. And whatever you meant about the gift, at any rate you respect us just as much as you do the continent ones, and didn't join in their humiliating song about the decaying body. You've given us women back our self-respect, for soul and body.

In their zeal for the faith some of our husbands had gone too far from the world and anything to do with the body, and we felt it. In other words, we found nothing more in them than a few bloodless ideas which they treasured as being particularly holy. We wives lack a deeper understanding of that kind of holiness. Then they treat us as though our bodies were disreputable, revolting, which make them dirty if they touch us. Or they fall on us as though we weren't there, as though our bodies had nothing

54

to do with us. Thank you, Paul. What you wrote about the body helps us. And if we feel that sometimes you express yourself in a rather wooden way, because you yourself haven't experienced this kind of love, we treat your words like a succinct prophetic saying which needs to be interpreted: 'The wife's body isn't hers to dispose of, but her husband's. Similarly, the husband's body isn't his to dispose of, but his wife's.' Anyway, it's a good thing that you wrote both sentences. For a long time only the first one applied to us. Nevertheless, there you do sound rather inexperienced in the things of love. So we shall fill your saying with the gift that God has given us, so that it can help those who love to love. And because you're anxious about the impending terrors of the end time, you should know that even when things get tough, two people who love each other can also give each other strength.

The sisters who have unbelieving partners also felt completely liberated. Some brothers had been taking it out on them because they were afraid that the sisters would pollute the church by continuing to live with their husbands. And of course the men whose wives are still outside are equally relieved. For example, Erastos will no longer have to pester his wife, because he knows that she's holy, even if she fights against baptism. That may perhaps open up her way to Christ better than anxiety and impatience. For me, Xenia, your good message was a real deliverance: 'The unbelieving husband is made holy by the believing wife.' I'm not desecrated, as some people thought, but he's made holy through me. The holiness of Christ is stronger than the impurity of the unbelievers. We really should have known that. We were too timid in our faith.

I, too, Leah, would love to have rejoiced with the others. But I can't. My husband can't come to terms with the fact that I belong to Christ. For him it's apostasy from the law of the fathers, betrayal of Moses and disobedience towards God. It's a miracle that he's put up with it so long. That's always given me hope. But now he recognizes only the one Israel, to which he belongs, and not the new Israel, to which we belong, so for him I'm an apostate. He'll turn me out, and I won't be able to stay with him. That's particularly hard for me, at the very time when you've taken away our doubts.

What you write about meat offered as sacrifices and temple festivals isn't very important for us. It's usually the men who go to the public receptions, and many of us really don't have the money to go into the shops and buy meat. Nor are we very often invited out by people who could afford a roast. However, the Timon affair oppresses us. Rufina would have loved to have been here, but her husband is so bad that she can't leave him alone. At night panic seizes him, and by day he's paralysed. We're worried about him. To that degree it was important that you appealed to the consciences of those who think themselves so strong. Not only about the meat, but also about the prostitutes.

However, Zinga and Mara have a question about that. Why do you say that men sin in their own body when they go to prostitutes? Why not in the prostitute's own body? Whose bodies are they turning into something to use? Their own or ours? Zinga and Mara know what they're talking about, and they aren't the only ones to have been abused by their owners. We'd very much like to talk to you about that when you come.

And one more thing: your abrupt attack on one of us. You know who we mean, the one who had a relationship with his father's young wife. We didn't like that. We don't want to excuse anything that's wrong. But we thought that the way in which you condemned him from afar, on the basis of a rumour, without making any attempt to discover what we made of the story, didn't become you. Some of us are also having misgivings. The men began to argue in the assembly immediately, and the person concerned quietly left. In the meantime he's died. He had an accident on a building site, fell off the scaffolding and broke his neck. So we couldn't talk to him again. I, Leah, know the woman and visited her, his father's young wife, his lover. She was out of her mind with grief. Certainly some things weren't right, but it's also wrong for people to point the finger at her. Some things look different when we sit with people and listen to them and feel their suffering. A snap judgment from afar doesn't do justice to that. And your hackneyed lists of vices don't help anyone. At most they serve those who build themselves up on the weaknesses of others, and support their own line by excluding sinners. Moreover you should note that the spirit gives the prophets among us insights into the depths of souls, that it reveals hidden things to us and brings to light what is concealed.

The night after the man we're talking about slipped away from our midst, I, Leah, had a prophetic dream which weighed heavily on my mind. I saw the body of Christ, his executed body, lying on the ground, torn and dismembered as though by wild animals. We struggled for a long time to interpret this image. Some people thought that it was an expression of my pain, because my husband had abandoned me. But I don't believe that. Others connected it with your first letter, in which you asked us – because of the rivalries among us – whether Christ was divided. But I'm certain that the vision was sparked off by the exclusion of this one brother. That passover night I saw a fanatical fire flame up in the eyes of some of the brothers and sisters. Not the illumination of the spirit of God, but a dark resolve to exclude and expel. And not just to drive the fallen into God's arms, as you probably think.

But let's tell you something else. We want to tell you straight out that we've caused offence in the church. That's because we've been faithful to what you handed down to us. Let me explain. We all learned from you that in the church of Christ all earthly status is abolished: 'There is no Jew and Greek, slave and free, male and female, for we are all one in Christ.'[82] In the last letter we told you that we'd been thinking about how we could take this really seriously. You responded to that in your letter, but only in connection with Jews and Greeks, slaves and free, and not in connection with men and women. You wrote that it didn't make much sense to change things now in a world which is coming to an end, i.e. for example to circumcise everyone or to free as many slaves as possible, because among us in Christ every slave is free and every free man or woman is Christ's property. You didn't write anything about us women. Of course we asked ourselves why. Have you forgotten us? Or did you think that the inequality between women and men is less important than that between Jews and Greeks?[83] Here we've come up against a contradiction which has really seemed strange to us for a long time, namely that we women can dress much more freely outside in worldly society than we can here at worship. Here everyone puts on her veil and covers her hair, while outside we walk through the streets with bare heads, without disturbing anyone. It may be that the women of Ephesus or Tarsus veil their heads in public – the Corinthian women are much freer about this.[84] It's not consistent to put on the veil of submission in the church of Christ, of all places. It seems as if Greek society understands things better: here are no male and female, all are one. Our men and some anxious sisters say that we should go on wearing some form of headscarf. That's how it's been from the beginning, they say, and it certainly has some deeper meaning. But we've learned from you to take the principles of our faith more seriously than any customs, simply because they've always been observed. To cut a long story short, we went to the assembly with bare heads, without any veils, and of course that annoyed the brothers tremendously. Not all of them; some thought that what we had done was worth thinking about, and young Jonah, Boaz's eldest, reported a story which he'd heard from Peter – do you know it? Jesus was invited to a meal by a pious man, and while they were eating and drinking, a woman forced her way into this male gathering, moistened Jesus' feet with her tears, loosened her hair and dried his feet with it. And Jesus didn't say to her, 'Be quick and cover your head again', but commended her before the angry men there for acting in faith.[85] Jonah heard that from Peter, and Peter himself had been there. And he said that he'd kept thinking of this woman when he first came here and saw so many women going around in the streets with bare heads.

At that point Boaz really let fly at his son and told him that he didn't know the whole story; the woman had been a prostitute, well known throughout the city, and Jesus had only defended her because he had a soft spot for the despised. He didn't mean all women to behave like prostitutes from then on. Nevertheless, we think that the story has a clear message for us. But as you see, we weren't all persuaded, though no one could think of a rational argument to the contrary. So the dispute resumed. Perhaps they'll appeal to you. That's why we prefer to write to you ourselves straight away, to tell you how things were. We're certain that you'll confirm that we were taking your line. In any case you'll accept that we're really thinking hard about the traditions which we learned from you. We often think of you and wish that you could be here.

Warmest greetings – wait, Mara has another problem – she also should have a word.

Yes, Paul, brother, thanks once again for your personal greeting. (It's Mara now.) I want to add one more comment on all this. I hope the others won't take offence, but I have to tell you. They're bothering about veils, as though one only had to throw away a bit of material and everyone would be equal at the Lord's table!

I can already see that what I'm saying is painful for them. And the way I'm saying it. It doesn't matter. You've got to be told. 'Not slave and free, not poor and rich.' That makes me laugh! Clearly the better-class gentlemen have been looked after for quite some time in the dining room when our kind comes rushing along. They eat lavishly, drink the finest wines. They're personally served by the staff as though it were a private banquet. They mix up the well-laid table of the master of the house with the Lord's table. So there's not much left for that. Hardly have the well-chewed bones been taken away than we arrive, the barmaids and the housemaids and the loaders and the cowgirls and all the others who can only get away when their work is done. I have to rush, wash up twice the plates in half the time, anxious whether my replacement will come in time – the landlord won't let me go unless I have a replacement – get ready quickly, rush down to the shipyard where Nannos works, say something nice to the manager so that they'll finally let him go, and then we pant up to Gaius' villa. Meanwhile some gentlemen have had a good meal and plenty to drink, and sit there talking business. They stare at us with a glazed gaze, and their songs remind me more of the bawling of drunkards. I feel as if I've gone from one pub to the next. And then they remark, 'So there you are! About time!'

If we're lucky, all that's left for the shared meal is a bit of bread and a sip of wine, and some gentlemen don't even have that because they're full and have drunk plenty. All the same at the Lord's table? Slaves and masters? Poor and rich? It's the same as everywhere else: the gents get the pick and we get the bits.[86]

That was Mara. You'll remember her, Paul. In a way she's right. There's a problem about starting together, and with those who have to come so late.

When are you coming, to talk about all this with us?

Phoibe sends greetings in the name of all the brothers and sisters of Kenchreai. She's come over specially to look after Fulvia. Phoibe will meet you at the harbour when you arrive. But first of all she'll take our letter and find a good ship and a reliable messenger.

Fulvia sends her greetings. Pray with us for her, that she may be delivered from her torments. Xenia and Leah send their greetings. We've taken it in turns to write. We greet you, and so do all the sisters of Corinth.

Peace be with you!

Paul and the brothers and sisters who are with me

to

all the sisters and brothers in Corinth

Grace be with you and peace!
Thank God that you've taken what I've written to you so well. It makes me happy to feel your faithfulness to the gospel of Jesus Christ which I brought to you, and also your faithfulness to me.[87] Indeed, I accept fully that you remember me in everything and are keeping to the traditions that I handed on to you.

However, I want you to be quite clear that the supreme head of every man is Christ, the supreme head of a wife is her husband, and the supreme head of Christ is God. If a man prays or speaks prophetically with his head covered, he disfigures his head. By contrast a woman disfigures her head if she prays or speaks prophetically without a veil. It's as if she'd been shaved. I think that if she doesn't want to wear a veil she should cut off her hair immediately. And if shorn hair or a bald head disfigure women, then they should wear their veils.

A man doesn't need a head covering. He is the image and glory of God. Woman is the glory of man. For the man didn't come forth from the woman, but the woman from the man. And the man wasn't created for the woman, but the woman for the man. So the woman must wear a covering on her head, also because of the angels.

That really means that in the Lord, there's no woman without man or man without woman, and just as the woman comes forth from the man, so of course the man comes into life from the woman, and both from God.

So now ask yourselves, is it proper for a woman to worship God with her head uncovered? Doesn't nature itself teach you that a long-haired man looks ridiculous, whereas people respect a woman with long hair? Her hair has been given to her as it were like a covering. But if people must have an argument – we don't have this custom, nor do any of the other churches of God.

But now I must give you some instructions, because things are getting steadily worse in your meetings rather than better, and I really can't accept that among you. For first of all, when the church assembles there are splits among you – I keep hearing about them and I partly believe it. But of course there must be some differences among you, so that it emerges which of you is fit.

What happens in your assemblies makes it impossible to eat the Lord's supper. For when you eat, everyone goes ahead with his own meal, so that one person remains hungry while another is already drunk. Don't you have your own homes to eat and drink in? Or do you despise God's church and are humiliating those who have nothing? What am I to say to you? Shall I accept your conduct? No, I certainly can't. For I received this tradition from the Lord, and also handed it on to you:

The Lord Jesus,
in the night
in which he was betrayed,
took bread,
gave thanks, and then he broke it
and said:
This is my body for you.
Do this in remembrance of me.

Likewise also the cup
after supper,
and said:
This cup is the new covenant
through my blood.
Do this whenever you drink of it,
in remembrance of me.

So whenever you eat this bread and drink of this cup, you make known the death of the Lord until he comes. Thus anyone who eats the bread and drinks of the cup of the Lord in a way which goes against the meaning of the supper[88] sins against the body and blood of the Lord. You should examine yourselves, and only after that eat the bread and drink of the cup.[89] For those who eat and drink without respecting the body of Christ[90] eat and drink judgment upon themselves. That's why many of you are sick and weak, and several have died. But if we judged ourselves critically, we wouldn't be judged. However, if we're now being judged by the Lord, we shall be put right with him, so that we shan't be condemned along with the world.

So, my brothers and sisters, when you come together to eat, wait for one another! If anyone is too hungry to wait, he should eat something at home, so that you don't provoke judgment for the way in which you meet.

I'll sort out the other matters when I come.[91]

Give my greetings to the sick Fulvia and her children. I think of her daily in my prayers. Greetings also to Phoibe, our colleague, and the church in Kenchreai. All the brothers and sisters from Ephesus send their greetings.

The grace of our Lord Jesus be with you, brothers and sisters.

Krispos, member of the church in Corinth

to

Paul, brother and kinsman

The Lord be with you!
Just so that there are no misunderstandings: Stephanas has my full confidence. What he reports to you will be a true account, and present all the questions in an unpartisan way. Nevertheless, at his express wish and at the suggestion of the community and indeed of Stephanas himself, I'm giving my own account of events and adding my own view. He'll confirm that to you. That by way of introduction.

You've led us to expect that you'll be coming soon and will sort everything out. Please do that, Paul. Everything has to be put straight here. Things are going astray all over the place and you must intervene on the spot, not from a distance through middlemen. That's also my objection to Stephanas' journey. I've nothing against his honourable intentions, but it won't help for him to look you up unless you intervene personally and create order. You can give Stephanas a letter; everyone is pleased when you write, but I fear that it will only spark off new discussions.

Take your last letter. You gave clear instructions to the women about how they're to dress in worship. There may be arguments over the reasons, but your instructions are clear. What do the sisters do? They mutter. They rebel. They pull your arguments to pieces. And you're a long way away. How are we to respond to their pedantic comments? 'Aha, he's contradicting himself,' Leah exults, with flowing hair:

> No woman without man,
> no man without woman;
> the woman comes from the man,
> the man from the woman;
> they both come from God,
> woman and man!
> That's it in Christ,
> no one has precedence.
> Well said, Paul.

She's picked a sentence from your letter and turned it into a taunt song. Old Karylla, Gaius' housekeeper, danced energetically through the assembly, tore her veil off her head, revealing her wispy hair, and shouted, 'My hair will hardly give the angels bad thoughts!' It was painful. And again we men couldn't think of anything to say.

Or take the second part, your instructions for orderly conduct at the supper. You speak to me from the heart. Our celebrations are threatening to get dissipated. What you wrote got to many people. They were terrified, confessed their thoughtlessness to those at a disavantage, and asked Mara and the other women slaves and workers from the harbour area to picture their distress. But when I wanted to strike the nail on the head and proposed an

63

order of worship which all were to observe, the arguments broke out again.

It wasn't really a dispute. If only they had disputed! I can cope with a dispute. No, the spirit itself – it sounds as though I'm accusing the Holy Spirit, God forgive me, but how else can I express what happened? The spirit seized Melas, the Egyptian, abruptly raised him to his feet, put a fiery gleam into his black eyes and bubbled from his mouth in human and heavenly tongues:

I am the way,
those who know, go the way.
Those who go the way, know.
Know whence, know whither.
No longer blind, no longer dumb.
I in God, God in me.

I understood that much, but only in fragments. I'm not sure whether I've got it down properly. It should have been translated, but the spirit leapt from Melas to Esther, from Esther to Phrygis, and from Phrygis to other brothers and sisters. Like a forest fire, it swept away everything we really needed: translation, interpretation, and even the careful ordering of worship. What can you do against the force of the spirit? What order can you bring when the spirit itself mixes everything up? And above all, what am I to do, standing there in amazement as the spirit carries others along? I've never had the gift of speaking in tongues. I've often prayed God for it, but in vain. I know the writings of the prophets and I can interpret them; I can be a tolerable teacher for brothers and sisters who want to use their understanding. I've prepared some people for baptism, and some have learned from me to call on Christ as Lord. But I've no command of the heavenly tongues. No wonder they don't listen to me when I make proposals to them in ordinary words. Simply because I express my own opinion and don't give them a revelation. You also express your opinion sometimes. Apparently that's too banal for saints. They look down on me from their lofty heights as if to say, Do you want to be a synagogue president[92] again? Do you want to fetter the spirit? That is, if they take any notice of me at all.

I sometimes doubt it. I doubt whether I'm really one of the saints. But even worse, I doubt the spirit. Can it throw the church into chaos? Is it really the spirit of God that is driving the brothers and sisters? Are they in fact one with God when they speak in tongues? Wrapped by his splendour, transformed into his form? Is this the way, as some of them say when they're drunk with the voices of angels?

Recently Lykos, seized by the spirit, in the midst of an uncontrolled flow of explosive syllables and fragmentary words, suddenly cried out, 'Out with Jesus! Jesus is cast out!', as he does when he's driving out harmful demons. As if he wanted to drive out Jesus like a tormenting spirit! Everyone was shocked, Lykos himself most of all. How can that happen? Can the spirit of God curse Jesus?

In the synagogue we used to pray for God to fulfil what he promised for the end of days: to pour out his spirit so that our sons and daughters would prophesy, the old would have dreams and the young see visions.[93] Now it's happening; the spirit is storming through the bodies of believers, visibly, indescribably, confusingly and – God forgive me – sometimes chaotically. In the synagogue, order prevailed when we met, ordered devotion. I had to ensure that one thing followed another. And I could do that well. I was in charge. I made it known that anyone who wanted to read, pray, sing or speak should indicate it to me. It was a blessing for everyone. They needn't hand things over to me here. Anyone who can do it should be nominated.

All the other associations round about have their regulations and their presidents. I don't want to take the godless clubs as an example, but I can't imagine our God being more disorderly than Aphrodite or Isis or Bacchus or whoever else they dedicate their drinking customs to.

Yes, unfortunately you're right. Our gatherings are getting steadily worse rather than better, and not just because of the supper. To be quite practical: we used to bring our sick to the assembly when they couldn't walk by themselves, and there was room and a quiet time for praying for them. Zinga and others, who felt that they had healing powers, laid hands on them. Lykos drove out the demons from heads and hearts. You know it yourself: that's how we behaved from the beginning. And we also organized the necessary ministries in the assembly. Anyone who needed care or help of some kind could make it known. There was room and time for it, and there were always capable brothers and sisters like Esther and Mattat and many others. All this has stopped. It's been diverted. Those who are filled with the spirit set the tone. They're 'on the way', and those who aren't personally drawn in are warmed by their glow. The rest gets lost. It becomes incidental. So people prefer to leave the sick at home, because no one takes any notice of them at worship. That's another reason, I think, why so many of us are getting sicker and sicker, as you so rightly point out.

I see it as my duty to point this out to the brothers and sisters. But no one listens to me. They listen to Stephanas. Some do, at any rate, those who go right back to the beginning, who have kept the church together with him. Stephanas nodded to all those who still had a clear mind, went with them into a side room where the chorus of spirit-filled voices was muffled, and revealed to us his decision to travel to Ephesus and look you up, along with Achaikos, his steward, and Fortunatus, his nephew. He said that there were business reasons for the trip, that he had to make some contacts in Asia and could take the opportunity of looking in on you. As though he could sell his raisins specially in Ephesus! No, like me he's worried about the church and wants to talk to you about it as soon as possible. He may sound out the market while he's there. His decision seemed a very sudden one to me. I can't get away so easily, and I would have liked to go with him.

I don't begrudge Achaikos the trip. He was beaming with pleasure when Stephanas disclosed his plan.

Paul, my brother, I've written much to you about my personal concerns and haven't even got to the theological questions I want to put to you. I'll do that tomorrow. Stephanas' ship isn't going until the day after.

Hannah, my grand-daughter, sends her warmest greetings. She's looking over my shoulder, and although she can't read, she knows that I'm writing to you. I should tell you that she and her friends would very much like to talk to you about veils, since what you wrote about them wasn't up to your usual level. I'm just telling you what they're saying. How does one reply? Tell them to shut up? Is it perhaps also an effect of the spirit that fourteen-year-old girls challenge us old men in such a disrespectful way? That's something else that never happened when I was president of the synagogue. Don't take her cheek the wrong way. I'm too fond of the child to be cross with her. Am I a fool?

The letter continues on p.72.

Paul, apostle through Jesus Christ and God, the Father, who has raised him from the dead,

to

all the beloved of God and those called to be saints, in Corinth and Achaia

Grace be to you and peace from God our Father and the Lord Jesus Christ!

First, I thank my God for all of you. I keep hearing how richly God has endowed you with his spirit and with the abundance of his manifold gifts. And I pray that your love may become even richer, that you may go to meet the Lord without fear, filled with the fruits of righteousness which Christ creates, for the glory of God.[94]

I don't want to leave you in any doubt, brothers and sisters, about the workings of the spirit.[95] You know how it was when you were still pagans, how irresistibly it pulled you towards the dumb idols. Perhaps that will help you to understand that no one who speaks through the spirit of God says 'Out with Jesus!'; and that no one can say 'Jesus is Lord' except by the Holy Spirit.

The gifts are distributed differently, but it's the same spirit. The tasks are distributed differently, but it's the same Lord. The effects are distributed differently, but it's the same God who brings about everything in everyone. Now the different manifestations of the spirit are given to individuals[96] for the use of all. For some are given the gift of speaking wisdom through the spirit, some are given knowledge in the same spirit, and others are given faith through the same spirit; yet others have gifts of healing through the one spirit, others powers, others prophecy, others interpretation[97] of the spirits, others different forms of speaking with tongues, others again the translation of speaking with tongues. All this is brought about by one and the same spirit: it gives everyone their special gifts at will.

For just as the body is a unity and at the same time consists of many members and organs, and though there are many parts of the body they are all one body, so too it is with Christ. We've all been baptized by one spirit into one body: whether Jews or Greeks, slave or free, we've all been given one spirit to drink.

The body doesn't consist of just one part, but of many. Though the foot might say, 'Because I'm not the hand, I don't belong to the body', it would still be part of the body. And though the ear might say, 'Because I'm not the eye I don't belong to the body', it would still be part of the body anyway. If the whole body were eye, what would become of hearing? If it were all ear, what would become of smelling? Now God has arranged members and organs as he wants to have each of them in the body. If the whole were one part of the body, what would become of the body? No, there are many members and organs, and one body. The eye can't say to the hand, 'I don't need you,' or the head to the feet, 'I don't need you.' Rather, we need the very organs of the body which seem to us particularly weak and sensitive; and we clothe all the more respectably the parts of the body which seem disreputable to us. Our unseemly parts get the most respectable clothing. The innocent parts of the body don't need this. God has made the body in such a way as to do greater honour to the lesser parts, so that there is no split in the body, but the members clearly care for one another. If one member suffers, all the members suffer with it, and if one member is honoured, all the members rejoice with it.

You're the body of Christ, and as individuals you're its members. And God has appointed some in the church first as apostles, secondly as prophets, thirdly as teachers; and then powers, gifts of healing, help, administrative tasks, different forms of speaking in tongues. Are all apostles? Or all prophets? Are all teachers? Do all have powers? Do all have gifts of healing? Do all speak in tongues? Can all translate?

Aim for the more important gifts! I'll show you a way which is far better than anything else.

If I speak in tongues,
human and angelic languages,
and have no love,
I'm like a noisy gong
or a clanging cymbal.

And if I have prophetic clairvoyance,
and know all mysteries and all knowledge,
and if I have all faith,
faith to move mountains,
and have no love,
I'm nothing.

And if I give away all I have,
even hand over my body,
myself, to be burned,
and have no love,
it's no use to me.

Love is patient.
Love is kind.
It isn't fanatical.
Love doesn't show off,
doesn't puff itself up,
isn't offensive.
It isn't out for itself,
it doesn't let itself get agitated,
it doesn't impute evil.
It doesn't delight in injustice,
it rejoices over the truth.

It bears all things.
It believes all things.
It hopes for all things.
It endures all things.

Love will never fade away.
Prophecies – they will be done away with.
Speaking in tongues – that will cease.
Knowledge – that will be superseded.
For we know imperfectly,
and we're imperfect prophets.

When the perfect comes,
the imperfect will be superseded.

When I was a child,
I spoke as a child,
I thought as a child,
I judged as a child.
But when I became a man,
I left childish things behind.

Yes, now we still see
enigmatically, in a mirror,
but then face to face.
Now I still know only fragments,
but then I shall know everything,
just as everything about me is known.

What now remain
are faith, hope and love,
these three.
And the greatest of them is love.

Follow love! And aim at the powers of the spirit, but above all to speak prophetically! For those who speak with tongues don't speak with other people, but with God. No one understands a thing; they speak mysteries through the spirit. But those who speak prophetically speak to others: they build them up, indicate critical points, console them. Those who speak with tongues build themselves up. Those who speak prophetically build up the community. I would very much like you all to speak with tongues, but I would much prefer you to speak prophetically. Those who speak prophetically are more important than those who speak with tongues, unless there's a translation, so that the community gets something out of it. Just suppose, brothers and sisters, that I came to you and spoke only in tongues – what good would that be to you? What if I didn't speak with you in the form of revelation or knowledge or prophecy or teaching? For a comparison in technique take a musical instrument, for example a flute or a lyre: if they don't produce any distinctive sounds, how can we know what tunes are being played? And if a trumpet gives an unclear signal, who will go into battle? It's the same with you over speaking with tongues. If you don't utter a single comprehensible word, how can anyone understand what you're saying? You're speaking into thin air.

Heaven knows how many different kinds of language there are in the world; but there's none that makes no sound. Now if I don't understand the meaning of the language in which someone is addressing me, I'm a foreigner to him and he's a foreigner to me. That also applies to you, as you aim for the powers of the spirit; acquire them to build up the church, so that you may be rich.

So those who speak in tongues should pray for the gift of being able to translate as well. For if I pray in tongues, my spirit prays, while my understanding remains unproductive. What follows from that? I will pray with the spirit, but I will also pray with the understanding. I will sing with the spirit, but I will also sing with the understanding. For if you only praise with the spirit, how can a newcomer say 'Amen' to your thanks, if he doesn't understand what you're saying? However splendid your prayer of thanksgiving may be, the other doesn't grasp any of it. I'm grateful to God that I speak in tongues more than all of you. But in the assembly I would prefer to say five words with my understanding, in order to involve others, than thousands of words in tongues.

Brothers and sisters, don't keep your understanding under wraps! Be immature over evil.[98] But be grown-up in your understanding. It says in the law,

> 'By people with strange tongues
> and through the lips of strangers,
> I will speak to this people,
> and even then they will not listen to me,
> says the Lord.'

That means that speaking in tongues is not only for believers but is also there to mark out unbelievers. By contrast, prophetic speech is not for unbelievers, but for believers. Just imagine the whole church gathering together, with everyone speaking in tongues, and then some newcomer or unbeliever arrives – won't they say, 'You're crazy'? But if an unbeliever or newcomer arrives and everyone speaks prophetically with him, they will all discover his weak points, they will find out what is burdening him. The secrets of his heart will emerge, and so he will fall on his face, worship God, and confess, 'Yes, truly, God is in your midst!'

So what about it, brothers and sisters? When you assemble, everyone has something to contribute: a song, a teaching, a revelation, speaking with tongues, a translation. Whatever it is, it should be done to edify. If there's any speaking in tongues, then each time it should be by two or at most three, one after the other, and someone should translate. And if there is no translator, then the person shouldn't speak. He should speak for himself, and for God. Two or three people should speak prophetically and the others should interpret. But if someone else sitting there has a revelation, the first should stop speaking. You can all speak prophetically one after the other, so that everyone learns and all are encouraged. And finally, the prophetic spirits are subject to the prophets. For God isn't a God of disorder, but of peace.[99] If someone thinks he's a prophet or filled with the spirit, then he should understand that what I'm writing to you is an instruction of the Lord's. If anyone doesn't recognize that, he won't be recognized.

So, brothers and sisters, aim at speaking prophetically, and don't close yourselves to speaking in tongues either. But do everything properly and in order.

The letter is interrupted. The continuation follows on p.76.

Krispos

to

Paul

Part Two

I hope, my dear Paul, that the bright new day will help me to get my thoughts in order, so that I can now get to the theological questions proper. But before I begin, I must tell you about another worry over organization which haunted me last night.

It's about the collection of money for the brothers and sisters in Jerusalem. It isn't the readiness to give that's the problem: on the contrary, since Titus told us about your plans, all of us here have agreed to take part. Indeed people are talking in grand style of the record sum which Corinth is going to contribute. They want to put all the other churches in the shade. But I can't see anyone taking any practical steps, and I'm afraid that one day you will arrive and nothing will be ready. I would very much like to see to it myself, but here again I'm prevented by the difficulty I've already described to you. The brothers and sisters have more important things on their minds and in their hearts than the trivial question how best to organize the collection of the gifts of money. They think that someone will organize that somehow, since there's such good will everywhere. What am I to do? How can I help you? As I understand it, the action is so close to your heart because relations with the Hebrew communities have to be stabilized, and in principle it's desirable for not only us Jews but also the Greeks to want to support you. But they don't get beyond wanting to, and the organization isn't there. Do give me some advice! I'll do anything in my power.

Now finally to the theological questions. Stephanas will also discuss them with you, and I know that he'll do so honestly and won't twist the truth. But he's a Greek, and the theological arguments of the Greeks are – shall we say – different from ours. At some points they find it difficult to see why we Jews should be tearing our hair. It's better for you to hear both sides.

I must go back a bit to explain myself. In the church we had an argument about the resurrection, or, as the Greek brothers and sisters put it, about eternal life. The occasion was the incident which I've already mentioned when Lykos, speaking in the spirit, uttered a curse against Jesus, 'Out with Jesus!' That's what everyone heard him scream; he himself heard the words coming out of his own mouth, and was as terrified as we were. No one could explain what had happened, least of all him. Then Chrysallis suddenly leapt to his support; at any rate, that's how I explain it to myself. She certainly wanted to help him, and in so doing sparked off a theological discussion which confused me even more than the uncanny event itself. I'll try and describe it to you as accurately as possible:

73

'You didn't curse Christ, but Jesus,' she said to Lykos, and it sounded as though she was comforting him, but I didn't understand what was meant to be comforting about what she said.

'Don't you understand?' said Chrysallis, still anxious about Lykos: 'He cast out Jesus, the earthly Jesus, whom God also cast out: "Cursed is the one who hangs on the tree"[100] – that's what's written. God rejected him and delivered him over to death. Just as he delivers over everything earthly to destruction. The spirit confirmed this through the mouth of Lykos.'

'No,' I exclaimed, quite upset by this interpretation, 'No! God never ever rejected Jesus. God raised him up and made him Lord of all. How can you say such a thing!'

Then Melas began to support Chrysallis' thesis with his Egyptian wisdom, and I have to confess that I find it terribly difficult to listen to him and respect him as a brother when he talks like this: 'You must make a distinction,' he lectured us, 'between the earthly Jesus and the Christ who is near to us in the spirit. Jesus, the bodily man, is a part of, an embodiment of, the world which has fallen victim to death. How can divine life have anything in common with decay? The spirit is life, Christ in us, infinitely far away from the abyss of rotting bodies and meaningless plagues. Christ, the Spirit, that's eternal life. God's living being, which was there long before the world, untouched by the corruptible. We can experience that. It fills us! Can't you feel it?'[101]

'Yes, but, but –,' Deborah, the flautist, struggled with the words: 'But the resurrection of the dead! Tell us what happens to the bodies of the dead if divine life and earthly fate have nothing in common? What happens to the resurrection then?'

And Melas answered, 'Resurrection of the dead? There's no such thing.'[102]

There was much to-ing and fro-ing that evening between Melas and the others without our getting any nearer to an agreement. Thank God, there were only a few who thought like Melas: for example, Lykos could make hardly anything of Chrysallis' interpretation and nothing at all of the theological concepts of the educated Greeks. But the more we struggled with their ideas, the more inexorably they questioned everything that supports our faith: they said that we were naive, because some of us imagined the resurrection of the dead as the prophet Ezekiel saw it:[103] with bodies of flesh and blood and bones and sinews. They raised acute questions like, 'What kind of body can it be that doesn't have death and corruption in it? Has anyone ever seen a body with eternal life? Do you love the world so much that you want to put God in it? What do you want more than to be one with God in the spirit?'

I kept thinking of sick Fulvia with her pains, and how she longed for the redemption of her body, and I was almost relieved – it may sound nonsense, but that's how I felt – relieved that she was too weak to come to the assembly and that she'd been spared all this. How could we have comforted her? And what does this kind of theology mean for people like her and me, who didn't feel the divine life in the spirit as overpoweringly as Melas and his friends? What's left of the promises, God's future for his people, if we're only concerned to experience the eternal in ourselves, which was always there?

I'm fairly knowledgable about the holy scriptures. But all my knowledge slipped through my fingers in this dispute. I'm confused by the way in which they use texts. For example, Chrysallis quoted Moses, 'Cursed is the one who hangs on the tree' – a passage I know very well. It plays a great role in the dispute with my old kinsfolk from the synagogue, and indeed for a long time I clung to it, since it was my weapon against you and the gospel before Christ overcame me. You'll remember. You showed me the true meaning of this saying: Jesus became a curse for us so that we might be free. I clung to that until today, and now Chrysallis gives the texts a different meaning, anyway – no matter what I quote, she and Melas and the other Greek brothers and sisters interpret it quite differently from me, and if they're feeling well disposed towards me, they simply laugh at the way in which I understand the scriptures, as one laughs at an old man who's no longer with it. I tell you, dear brother Paul, it causes me a lot of trouble. And here I'm thinking not only of myself but of you and the whole church and of how I can hold it together. Too many preachers go through here; they all have something to say; each brings yet more theological ideas. No wonder that everyone constructs the kind of theology that suits them. Those snoopers from Syria have started something else. Not that they made any theological statements – they simply listened to the people. But their questions have evidently led some of the brothers and sisters to think that your authority isn't the last word. I must say that this disturbs me a great deal.

Sometimes I also think of Apollos. It would be important and useful for him to visit the church too. He's close to the Greeks: he knows their thought-world, he speaks their language, he has a command of their novel methods of interpreting scripture. Some people have learned from him. Not these theories about the resurrection – I don't want to impute anything doubtful to Apollos. On the contrary, it would be really good if you could persuade him to come to Corinth and explain some things to his people. But above all, come yourself. We need your clear mind and strong hand.

Greetings to Sosthenes, my old friend and colleague, when he gets back to you. I assume that he's travelling for the kingdom of God, otherwise he would surely have sent greetings. Greetings also to Prisca and Aquila, her husband, and all who went with them to Ephesus.

How have things turned out for you? Are you still exposed to the same ugly machinations? God protect you!

I, Krispos, greet you with my signature.

Shalom!

Paul

to

the church in Corinth:

continuation of the letter[104]

Brothers and sisters,
I want to make clear to you the gospel which I brought to you and which you also received. You stand in it and you will also be saved through it. I want to do this in the very words with which I

brought it to you – if you remember – otherwise you'd have begun to believe in a completely mindless way. For from the beginning on, I've handed down to you this tradition which was also handed down to me:

Christ
died for our sins
as the scriptures bear witness,
and was buried.
And he was raised on the third day
as the scriptures bear witness,
and appeared to Cephas,
then to the Twelve;
after that he appeared
to five hundred brothers and sisters all at once

– most of them are still alive, but some have since died –

after that he appeared to James,
then to all the apostles.

Last of all he also appeared to me, as it were to a 'freak', since in fact I'm the last of the apostles, and don't deserve to be called an apostle because I persecuted the church of God. But by God's grace I am what I am, and his grace which was at work in me wasn't in vain, but I worked hard, more than all of them. Not I, however, but the grace of God did it with me. Still, whether I or the others did it, that at any rate is how we pass on the message and that's how you began to believe.

Now if Christ has been made known as the one who has been raised from the dead, how can some of you say 'There is no such thing as resurrection of the dead?' If there's no resurrection of the dead, Christ hasn't been raised either. And if Christ hasn't been raised, then our message is empty, and so too is your faith. In that case we're shown up as false witnesses to Christ, because we have borne witness that God has raised Christ – whom he hasn't raised at all, if the dead can't be raised. For if the dead can't be raised, then Christ hasn't been raised either. But if Christ hasn't been raised, then your faith is worthless, and you're still stuck in your sins. Indeed, in that case all those who have died in Christ are also lost. If we've hoped in Christ only in this life, we're more wretched than anyone else.

But Christ has risen from the dead. He's the first, before all the dead.

Dying also began through one man – just as the resurrection of the dead began through one man. For as all die in Adam, so all will be made alive in Christ. But each in turn: first of all Christ, then on his coming all who belong to Christ. Only then does the end come, when Christ hands the government back to God the Father, after he's abolished every form of rule with all its power and violence. For he must reign until

'he has put all his enemies under his feet'.

The last enemy to be disarmed will be death. For

'God has subjected all things to him'.

'Subjected all things' here obviously means everything but God himself, who has subjected them to him. So when everything has been subjected to him, he himself, the Son, will also submit to him, to the one who has subjected all things to the Son, so that God is all in all.

Otherwise what are people doing who are baptized vicariously for the dead? If no dead are raised at all, why are they being baptized for them? And why do we expose ourselves to such dangers, hour by hour? Day after day I'm dying. Yes, truly, brothers and sisters, as truly as you're my pride and joy in Christ Jesus our Lord! What do I gain from having fought with wild beasts in human form in Ephesus? If the dead aren't raised, then 'Let's eat and drink, tomorrow we're dead.'

Don't fool yourselves: bad company undermines good habits![105] Get your common sense back, so that you don't sin. Some of you have no idea of God. Shame on you!

But now someone may say, 'So how are the dead raised? With what kind of body do they come?' Stupid! When you sow something, it isn't brought to life without dying. And what you sow, you don't put into the ground in the form which it will take, but as bare grain – wheat, for example, or something else. But God gives it a shape in accordance with his plan, and he gives each seed its own shape. Not all living beings have the same body:

human bodies are different from animal bodies, the bodies of birds from the bodies of fishes. And then there are heavenly bodies and earthly bodies, but the heavenly bodies look quite different from the earthly bodies. Sunshine is quite different from moonlight, and starlight is different from both of these. Indeed, even one star shines differently from another. It's the same with the resurrection of the dead; it's sown in a frail state and it's raised completely whole. It's sown as an insignificant thing and it's raised in splendour. It's sown in weakness and it's raised in power. Body and soul are sown, and a body is raised which is shaped and given a soul by the spirit of God.[106]

If there's this life with body and soul, then similarly there can be a new life brought about by the Spirit of God. And that's what is written:

'Man – the first Adam –
became a living soul.'

But the last 'Adam' became a life-giving spirit. However, what the spirit of God creates wasn't there from the start, but only this life with body and soul – what the spirit will create comes afterwards. The first is human beings made from the earth, earthly. The second is human beings from heaven. All earthly beings are created like the earthly Adam, and all heavenly beings are created like the heavenly Adam. Just as we've borne the image of the earthly Adam, so too we shall bear the image of the heavenly Christ.

I want to tell you this, brothers and sisters: flesh and blood can't simply take over God's kingdom as an inheritance; the corruptible doesn't simply inherit incorruptibility. Look, let me tell you a mystery: we shall not all die. But we shall all be changed, in a flash, in a moment, at the last signal from the trumpet. For:

The signal will sound,
the dead will be raised
to life incorruptible,
and we shall be changed.

For this fragile existence must slip into unbroken life, and this mortal life must put on immortality like a garment. When that's happened, when this fragile existence slips into unbroken life and this mortal life is wrapped in immortality like a garment, then what the saying describes will happen:

Death is swallowed up in victory.
Death, where is your victory?
Death, where is your sting?[107]

Thanks be to God. He gives us the victory through our Lord Jesus Christ. So, my beloved brothers and sisters, hold firm! Nothing must upset you. Do your utmost, as always, working for the Lord. You know that your efforts aren't in vain.

Now about the collection for the saints in Jerusalem. You should follow the arrangements I made for the churches in Galatia. Every Sunday you should put aside whatever you can afford. That means that the collecting won't have to wait until I come. When I arrive, I will send messengers, whom you must choose, with credentials to Jerusalem, to deliver your contribution. If it seems appropriate for me to go, too, they can travel with me.

I shall come to you via Macedonia. I want to go through Macedonia once more, and then perhaps I will stay with you, possibly even over the winter, so that you can set me on my way when I continue my journey. I don't want to see you just in passing. I hope to spent some time with you, if the Lord allows it. I shall remain in Ephesus until Pentecost, since a wide and effective door has opened to me, and I have many opponents.

If Timothy arrives, see that he doesn't have to worry. He does the Lord's work just as I do. Don't let anyone underestimate him. Send him on his way in peace so that he gets back to me, since I and the brothers and sisters are longing to see him.

As for brother Apollos, I've often asked him to come to you with the brothers, but he's not prepared to do so at the moment. But he will come when it suits him better.

Be watchful, stand firm in the faith, bravely and strongly. Let everything that is is done among you be done in love.

I have one more matter for you, brothers and sisters. You know Stephanas and his household, and you know how everything that has happened in Achaia began with them, and that they've taken responsibility for the saints. Please do what they say, and what you're told by all their colleagues and those who are making an effort. I'm very glad that Stephanas, Fortunatus and Achaikos have come here. They've filled in the gaps, since I'm not there.[108] They've reassured me, and you as well. You should listen to such people!

The churches in Asia send their greetings; in particular Aquila and Prisca greet you in the Lord, along with the church in their house. All the brothers and sisters greet you. Greet one another with the holy kiss.

Here's my greeting with my own hand, Paul.

If anyone does not have love for the Lord, let him be expelled.[109]

Maranatha!

The grace of the Lord Jesus be with you.

My love to you all in Christ Jesus.

The church of the Corinthians, represented by Erastos, Xenia and Tertius,

to

Paul, our brother, still in Ephesus

Grace be with you!

We've been wanting to write to you for a long time, and we're grateful for your long letter and the greetings which Stephanas, Fortunatus and Achaikos have brought from all of you. However, first, from what you told us we expected you to pay us a personal visit soon after Pentecost – evidently you've been detained by other commitments – and secondly, things have happened here which preoccupy us and concern us immeasurably, so that your letter has faded into the background. Now the church has finally decided to send you a reply and tell you in Ephesus above all about the marvellous events which have completely changed our church. The three of us said that we were ready to write to you about them in the name of the whole church, and we've been commissioned to do so. Stephanas wanted to be involved, but unfortunately he's not feeling too well today, and we didn't want to put it off yet again. However, we hope that in the meantime Timothy has passed on our greetings to you and everyone else. He spent the night with us on his way back from the churches in the province, shortly before Stephanas returned, and we found him a ship. We hope that everything has gone well with you.

Now back to your letter. Stephanas and his people were welcomed with great expectations: everyone had come, and even Fulvia, almost at death's door, had herself brought to the assembly – it was the last time that she was with us. She's now died.

Those who had come back had so much to tell us that they didn't get round to reading out your letter immediately. Fortunatus gave an impressive account of the difficult circumstances in which you were working in Asia. He gave a description of the laborious chores you had to do, and told us how often your work was put in question by setbacks; how anxiety about the unpredictable interventions by the authorities had led to the loss of a number of brothers and sisters, how you yourself kept being slandered and had to justify yourself to the security forces, and how all this was getting you down and damaging your health. We never stop praying for you.

Of course we also heard the good things: how the churches in the houses stick together and support one another, and how despite all the dangers they keep winning over new brothers and sisters. Achaikos was very enthusiastic about the house church meeting with Prisca and Aquila. It made him happy to embrace old friends like Sosthenes, Silvanus, Apollos and of course you above all. He didn't want to stop telling us all about it. But Stephanas impatiently pressed your letter into his hand and said that it was more important than all the stories. So Achaikos read it out.

What you wrote made sense to everyone, and it was certainly a good thing that you reminded us of the unity of the church, though your concerns are now out of date. Since Pentecost there have been no more disputes. The church is now more solid than ever.

There were discussions about your remarks on the resurrection of the dead, but only later: some people talked about it after

Fulvia's burial and raised critical questions. And the reading of your letter was interrupted once. Nannos, the 'dwarf', felt something and indicated it painfully and at the same time comically. At any rate, this was the only disruption during the readings. After your great poem about love, Nannos suddenly sprang up and stood there, hands on hips, as though he wanted to give a speech, but he kept silent and stared into heaven. Achaikos went on reading your remarks about speaking with tongues and comprehensible language: 'If you don't utter a single comprehensible word, how can anyone understand what you're saying? You're speaking to thin air!' Just as he got to that point, Nannos burst out, speaking with tongues, or rather he shouted and cried out, trembled, clenched his fists, babbled and whimpered; it sounded like the angry crying of a baby at last picked up after an eternity, after endless waiting. No one could translate it. Everyone was silent, overwhelmed by the weight of this outburst. Only Deborah responded the crying of the 'dwarf' with her flute, reflecting it with shrill tones, gently translating it into soft sounds, and Nannos sank back into his place, shaken by vigorous weeping, his face wet with tears.

That was the last time that Deborah played the flute in the worship. A new tone prevails in our gatherings, and those who've set it have also brought new musicians with them: they play splendidly, with double flutes and all kinds of percussion, so Deborah has yielded her place to them.

But back to your letter. As I said, there was an argument about dying and new life, and the occasion was Fulvia's funeral. You should know that Fulvia had an agonizing death. The sisters who were with her day and night were there, and told us all about it. It wasn't agonizing just because her body was racked with pain. She'd borne that for a long time with amazing bravery. But her soul was also tormented about dying: she struggled, she was afraid, she groaned and raged against the decay of her body. She clung to this life and cursed God for destroying it for her. Indeed we have to say – without wanting to speak ill of her – that she seemed to love this earthbound bodily life, and felt no relief when we told her that at last she would be free of it.

People talked about that when we buried her. And those whom you called stupid over the question of the resurrection of the dead and who still kept quiet when your letter was being read out now made themselves heard. 'If that kind of thing happens,' said Melas, 'what's all this teaching about the resurrection of the dead worth? Evidently it only leads to the soul clinging to the worn-out body in senseless panic instead of casting it off like a tattered garment, instead of going into the open air from a dilapidated hut. Any philosopher can teach us how to despise death in a cheerful and relaxed way, free from anxiety and groaning.[110] Are the wise of this world to put us to shame? Us who have endless life in the spirit?'

That's how Melas talked, and many people told him to keep quiet, now, when everyone was mourning Fulvia. But the critical question which he'd raised wouldn't rest, even more after most recent events. Isn't the hope that you preached to us strong enough to drive out anxiety? It's a question of results. What's the effect of your gospel, Paul? Does it make people confident or anxious? Does it create doubt or give assurance? Does it imprison us behind the walls and bars of this world, or does it open up God's light? So far we've never asked such radical questions. Now we must raise them, and put them to you.

For apostles of Christ have come to us whose effect is different from yours.[111]

They reached Corinth shortly before Pentecost, a group of men, Jews of different origin, younger than you, but very mature and full of inner power. They've already achieved amazing things in other churches. That's clear from the letters of commendation which they use for their credentials as apostles. For example, the church of Pergamon[112] confirms their amazing powers: the sick have been healed, the eyes of the blind have been opened, demons have taken flight, stubborn unbelievers have been reached by the rays of God's light. The church of Thyatira praises the power of their sermons and the indescribable experiences that they lead to: experiences of the deepest union with God, the bliss of security and enthusiastic gratitude. We needn't list all the commendations for you; in the meantime we've been able to confirm all this, since it's happening in our midst as a result of their activity. So without their having to ask us, we've written them similar letters of commendation for the country churches in Achaia. For it's their task to bring this special light of the gospel from Corinth to everyone.

They preached for the first time in our church at Pentecost. As true Israelites, they said, they wanted to direct our thoughts to the place on which all the descendants of Abraham dwell at this festival: the revelation of God on the holy mountain.[113] And they presented Moses to us as we'd never seen him before – not as one of us, either Greek or Jew. This was Moses as he's understood only with the eye of the spirit: Moses the model of the man of God, with a beauty which already marked him out in childhood as one who was loved by God, a wisdom which combined all the wisdom of all peoples and yet far surpassed it; the power of his deeds, signs and wonders; the power of his words, words of life, received from God and marked out by him, chiselled indestructibly on stone tablets, as an eternal message for humankind. Indeed, Moses spoke with God as if with his friend: his place was above the people, high above with God, and death stayed away from him, since God transported him and took him to himself.[114] Anyone who looked at him saw the fiery gleam of God, and the divine splendour permeated him and transformed him.[115] We've all experienced this. This is the Moses who foresaw Christ and said to the Israelites: 'The Lord your God will raise up a prophet like me.'[116]

And while they were painting the miraculous figure of Moses before our eyes, their faces became bright and shining, as if they were angels, and we saw it; everyone saw how the heavenly splendour of Moses was reflected on their faces. And they said to us, 'Come, let's ascend the mountain of God with Jesus, towards the holy light.' For they told us how Jesus took some select disciples with him and climbed the mountain,[117] higher and higher, to the point where Moses spoke with God. And they took our souls as it were by the hand and led us up with them, and they themselves changed, towards the divine splendour, and were beside themselves with bliss. The dark valleys, the dull business of this world, bodies with their suffering, were forgotten: they took us upwards, towards the light; the heavens were open and we felt how everything had been left behind, had become unimportant, had fallen away from us. Nothing held us any more. There, on the summit of the holy mountain, Jesus was standing in the divine splendour alongside Moses, transfigured as he was, bathed in unspeakable light. And caught up in the ecstasy of the apostles, carried up into dizzy heights and yet deeply immersed in God, we all saw it. No one could resist it. Only Mara — evidently she couldn't bear the holiness of the hour, so she kept chattering in her crude way: 'Should I perhaps build a few huts up there so that the gentlemen can make themselves at home?' That was out of place, but no one held it against her at that moment. Indeed, we weren't even embarrassed, so overpowering was the feeling that came over us. Even the children didn't make a sound; they, too, were in the grip of something that they barely understood, indeed something which went beyond the understanding of any of us. Some people worshipped, others sat as though in a dream, some had sunk to the ground and lay there, bewitched by the ineffable.[118] Little Phrygis kept dancing with half-closed eyes in the midst of the throng, as though she were floating towards Christ.

And then there were the signs and wonders. Here a woman who had been hobbling around on crutches jumped up, stretched herself, shook her legs, danced and hopped. There a man rubbed his eyes and looked around him in amazement; he was an old man, long blinded, and now saw God's light. A girl, deformed with a rash for years, praised the Lord with a smooth complexion. Here and there among the visitors demons cried out, raged, and tried to get away. Timon too: unable to go out of the house for weeks, he had dragged himself there, supported by Rufina, and had pinned all his hopes on the apostles and the great deeds they were credited with in the letters. He's been healed. Since Pentecost, nothing has tormented him in the night again. The apostle just looked at him, the biggest of them, who had portrayed Moses for us. He looked steadily and deeply into his eyes. No ifs and buts, no talk, not a bit of uncertainty. But there was assurance, authority and a spirit of faith which does wonders.

That's what happened, and it's only the beginning, because it keeps on happening among us through the authority of these missionaries. And though we're all first beginners compared with them, what we've experienced is powerful enough to give us a thirst, a burning thirst, for complete union with God. There's no one who doesn't feel it; these men are ambassadors of Christ, and they perform their commission with unprecedented spiritual power. That's obvious. They radiate an assurance which quenches any doubt. Everything becomes clear, unquestionable, settled. There's no need for any more dispute. The time of dissension is over.

All this is miraculous, almost indescribable, difficult to communicate to someone who hasn't experienced it in person. Only one thing oppresses us: the new experiences put us somewhat at a loss where you're concerned. What now are we to make of what you've offered us, you and Silvanus and Timothy and anyone else working with you? To put it bluntly: it didn't have the splendour which is now overwhelming us. The new apostles have something – it's hard to put into words, but at any rate you didn't have it. What does that mean? Didn't you have a commission to bring God's light in all its fullness? Or did you deliberately hold some things back? Did you cover up the complete gospel out of fear that it might blind us? Did you in fact treat us like children, who are kept from certain things? We recall that you once wrote something like that. But why? Why so narrow? Give us your reasons, and then perhaps we can understand them! Talk is going round among us that you simply weren't big enough for it: too little spirit of faith, too little assurance, too little of the divine splendour. What are we to say to this kind of talk?[119] The arguments develop and what young Fortunatus reports about conditions in Ephesus makes it even more difficult to counter such a lack of respect. Evidently you're not all that competent: your work seems to us to be clumsy and laborious; for more than two years you've been creeping between small gains and humiliating setbacks; the confidence of the brothers and sisters in Asia is badly shaken. You haven't had a convincing success. Are you at the end of your tether? Fortunatus told us worrying things about your state of health, about the convulsions which keep throwing you to the ground, and also about serious illnesses among your colleagues. Here people get better. Here competent apostles are at work. Their gospel is convincing. Its effect is obvious. Don't get us wrong. We're writing to you because you're important to us. We all want to feel that you have God's power. But you must show us what you're capable of.

We very much hope that this letter reaches you in Ephesus. (Though to be honest, we hope even more that you're already on the way to us, to counter all the uncertainties here.) 'If the Lord allows it,' you write. Yes, may Christ allow it soon. And we hope things don't go wrong because you're delaying, dear Paul.

Erastos, Xenia and Tertius the secretary greet you in the name of everyone.

Peace be with you.

Karylla, housekeeper of Gaius

to

Paul, the dear apostle, in Ephesus

Grace and peace to you and all who are with you!
I'm sure you still remember me, dear Paul. I'm old Karylla, one of Gaius' household staff. You didn't baptize me like Gaius, my master; at that time I was still undecided. But you were often with us. I've prepared meals for you and poured you wine. Since then I've been a member of the church for a long time. And since Gaius lost his wife, I've been housekeeper here.

He knows nothing of this letter. It's the first time that I've done anything behind his back. But in this case it's better.

The talk that goes on in our house gives me no rest. It's in a small group, after the assembly. They go on sitting there for a while: the new apostles and a select group of admirers. Of course Melas is there, and Timon, from whom they drove out the demon of horror. And Phalakros, who's glad because he had led Timon astray and caused his panic. Then there's Titius Justus, the shoemaker, from whom you once rented a room; Mattat, who's kept emphasizing that we belong only to Christ; Krispos, too, who was often envious because he himself couldn't speak with tongues. Now it's caught hold of him and he enthuses about the 'real leaders' and the 'tangible unity of the church'; and a few more. They all listen attentively to the words of the great apostles regardless of whether what they say is good or just shabby. It looks to me like a nest of conspirators, the court of the new rulers, or something like that. I don't say anything when they talk about the gospel or about everyday problems. But they also talk about you. And not subtly. I hear that when I pour the wine for them. Free of course. They don't hesitate to eat and drink and have themselves served at our expense. They take no notice of me, so I can have a good listen. As you know, servants are really nobodies. The masters are so to speak by themselves and speak quite openly. I serve the fruit and listen. But it hurts me inside, the way they talk. And Gaius, my master, sits there silently. As the host he's good at doing the right thing by all the guests. I don't know what's going on in his head.

I think you have to know about it. Usually it begins with someone enthusing: 'That was another experience, out of this world, it was never like that before. No one has ever presented the gospel to us so clearly, so radiantly, without any distortions.' They've already started comparing. They avoid mentioning your name; even the apostles act as though they didn't know what you were called. But the talk is constantly about you. Anyone who has an ear can hear it. For example, Krispos says, 'What fullness, what power!' Phalakros joins in: 'Just think what poor Timon would have been spared if these miracles had happened earlier.' Then Mattat explains to the apostles, 'Before you came, a lot of it was really pathetic.' And Timon, 'Other people weren't capable of bringing what you've brought us,' and Melas, 'Didn't they have enough authority? Didn't they understand their commission properly?' And finally Titius Justus: 'Perhaps they didn't have a proper commission.' All this to these new preachers, as though it were their job to check your competence and evaluate your actions. Moreover that's precisely what they are doing. Not openly and directly, but anyone who has ears . . .

'There are people . . .,' they go on to say, 'even among those who work for the gospel, there are people,' they say, 'who overestimate themselves. They feel called to a task for which they simply don't have the spiritual power. Anyone with clear judgment,' they say, 'can immediately see that their worldly wisdom isn't enough. They may understand some things in a worldly way,[120] but this is a divine commission. They don't ask themselves whether there mightn't be be something wrong with their commissioning. They're only surprised that no one commends them any more. And so they begin to commend themselves, to mention their own names, to chat people up so that they have at least some of them on their side.'

'The old story,' Titius Justus nods in great excitement. 'On their own initiative, at their own expense. They've commissioned themselves because they couldn't get a commission in Antioch.'

'They've ambitious plans,' say the great apostles, and everyone hangs on their words, 'and perhaps they have good will, but they've only ever come to know Christ in a worldly way, so they can only talk about him in a worldly way.'

'Now we know Christ in quite a different way,' exclaims Mattat with shining eyes. 'We know him in God's way, in the spirit and in truth. Thank you.'

'In the end these people are fighting only for their own recognition,' say the spiritual gentlemen, who have evidently left the ways of the world far behind them, 'and as a result their gospel has become dull, their appearance without splendour, their work questionable. Nothing comes across any more, no fire of the spirit, only words, words of dull worldly reason. And because in some way they probably sense their deficiencies, they tend to go on at the gullible with doubtful rhetorical tricks. They think that they could even pull the wool over God's eyes.'

Now everyone laughs, and the gentlemen start up again, 'They get involved in obvious deceptions,' they say, 'take money out of people's pockets and enrich themselves: a poor substitute for a loss of importance they can't reconcile themselves to. A despicable game!'

Then Titius once again, even more agitated, 'I suspected it! I've always suspected it! And the brothers from Syria said it too!'

Paul, my dear, some people from the church are beginning to suspect you of evil things. And these apostles lean back, accept another glass of wine, without paying, of course, and sum up: 'The task is a great one, but who is called for it? Christ needs workers for his field, but who is competent for it? Not everyone, that's obvious. Not everyone is fit for the gospel. It really would be better if such people gave up and kept quiet. Better for them, better for all those who fall into the snares of such deceivers, better for the church.'

That's how these people talk, my dear Paul, and there's no one there to shut them up. No, everyone nods 'Yes' and 'Amen', and 'How good it is that you're here.' This is what you should know. I'm telling it to you secretly, behind Gaius' back. Gaius doesn't play the same tune as Titius or Phalakros or Melas. But he keeps quiet. It's probably difficult for him as host to say anything to his guests, especially when everyone sits at their feet.

I'm often with you in my prayers. Come to us soon. Otherwise some people will forget how much we owe to you and your people.

Achaikos sends you his warmest greetings. He helped me to write this. I also send greetings from Quartus. He's taking care of the letter for me. To send it I have to pay more than I've really got. So I'm taking some of the money I put by for the Jerusalem collection. Don't be cross with me. I'll save up again, until you come and take it away.

May the love of Christ preserve you from all evil!

Paul, apostle, commissioned by Jesus Christ, and his colleagues Titus, Silvanus and Timothy,

to

the church in Corinth

Grace be with you and peace from God our Father and the Lord Jesus Christ!
Some people have descended on you and made a powerful impression on some of you, so that we fear that you could in fact regard us as incapable workers, who would do better to keep quiet and give up.[121] But thanks be to God, who in Christ still has us in his triumphal procession,[122] and who fills all the world with the fragrance of his knowledge through us. Indeed, we are the healing fragrance of Christ for God, among those who are to be saved and among those who are being lost: for some a deadly fragrance, the smell of death, and for others a living fragrance, the breath of life. Furthermore, indeed, 'who is competent for this?'

We certainly aren't. Not like the many who peddle the word of God. We speak bluntly, in a way which comes from God, God responsible in Christ.

Are we again already beginning 'to commend ourselves'?[123] Or do we need, as some people do, letters of commendation to you or from you? You are our letter of commendation, written in our hearts. All people can read it and understand it. It is, after all, obvious that you are a letter of Christ, prepared by us, not written with ink but with the spirit of the living God, and not on tablets of stone but on tablets of human hearts.

Yes, that is what the assurance that we have looks like. We have it through Christ; we have it before God. Not that we're capable by ourselves of judging something as if it came from ourselves. No, our competence comes from God. He has made us competent: as those commissioned[124] for the new covenant, not of the letter, but of the spirit. The letter kills, but the spirit gives life.

Now if that commission of death,[125] letters carved in stone,[126] has its splendour – as is well known, the Israelites couldn't look Moses in the face 'because of the splendour on his face', which disappeared again – then the commission of the spirit will be even more full of splendour. For if the commission of condemnation already had its splendour, the commission to speak out freely will be even more radiant. Indeed, what was splendid there pales completely before this splendour, which exceeds everything. For if something that was coming to an end was already splendid, how much more splendidly will what remains shine out![127]

That is what the hope that we have looks like. So we can speak with great openness, and not like Moses, who 'put a covering over his face'[128] so that the Israelites couldn't see how it ultimately faded. Rather, their senses have been turned to stone: to the present day this very cover has remained over the Old Testament when they read it, and no one takes it off; for it will be taken off only by Christ. To the present day a covering has lain over their hearts whenever Moses is read. But,

'as soon as they turn to the Lord,
the covering will be removed.'[129]

To the 'Lord': that means, to the spirit. And where the spirit of the Lord is, there is freedom. We all see in a reflection[130] with uncovered face the splendour of the Lord, and by this we shall be transformed into this image, from light to light of a kind that only the Lord makes, the spirit!

That is the commission that we have through God's mercy, and so we don't give up. But we keep our distance from all insidious manipulation, we use no tricks, nor do we play any false games with the word of God. We speak openly and we speak the truth: in this way we commend ourselves to the judgment[131] of all men and women in responsibility before God. If our gospel is nevertheless covered, then it is covered among those who are being lost, where the God of this age has darkened the sense of unbelievers, so that they don't see how the gospel makes the splendour of Christ shine out. He is the image of God. We don't proclaim ourselves, but Christ Jesus as the Lord! At most we proclaim ourselves as your slaves, for Jesus' sake. For God who said, 'Let the light shine out of the darkness', has filled our hearts with light, so that we may bring to light what we know: the radiance of God on the face of Christ![132]

But we have this treasure in fragile containers, so that the overwhelming power comes from God and not from us. We're under pressure from all sides, but not oppressed; in difficulties, but not in despair; hunted, but not done for; forced to the ground, but not lost. We constantly carry the killing of Jesus around with us in our own bodies, so that the life of Jesus also becomes visible in our body. Living, we're constantly hurled into death for Jesus' sake, so that the life of Jesus may also shine forth in our dying existence. That's how we feel death, and you feel life!

Here we have the same spirit of faith as we find in a saying from scripture,

'I have believed and so I have spoken.'

That is how we too believe, and so we too speak, because we know that the one who has raised up the Lord Jesus will also raise us up with Jesus and present us together with you before him. Yes, it's for your sake that everything is taking place, so that grace will unfold and incite more and more people to overflowing gratitude, to the glory of God.

So we don't give up. On the contrary, although we're worn down outwardly, inwardly we're renewed day by day. What torments us for the moment is hardly important, but it does create for us a wealth of final glory, beyond anything imaginable. What we have in view is nothing visible, but something which can't yet be seen; for what one can see is provisional. What can't yet be seen is final. For we know that when our earthly existence, this tent, is torn down, we have a building from God, a house not made with hands, a final one, in heaven. We're still in this tent, and groan, we long so to speak to put on our heavenly dwelling straight away, like a coat. We don't want to stand there naked if we have to take off the earthly. Indeed, as long as we still live in the tent, we groan; we find things difficult, because we don't want to go out. We'd prefer to be overdressed, so that what is mortal is swallowed up by life. But God himself has already prepared us for that by giving us the spirit as an advance on the new life. So we're always full of confidence, and that's because we know that even if we have a home here in the body, if we're living in a foreign land, far away from the Lord – for we go about in faith and not yet in sight – we're full of confidence, and so we really would much prefer to go from the body to the Lord and be at home with him. That's why we also think it vitally important to do his will, whether at home or abroad. For we must all appear before the judgment seat of Christ, where it will become clear what each person will receive, depending on what he or she has done in this earthly life, good or evil.

So because we know what it means to fear the Lord, we 'chat up people'; but to God it's obvious who we are. And I hope that it's become evident to your judgment who we are. We aren't commending ourselves to you again, no, but we're giving you arguments to put us in the right light, so that you have something to use against those who are outwardly impressive, but inwardly have nothing to be proud of. We, too, have already been in ecstasies, but if we have, it's been for God. For you we prefer to keep a clear mind. For the love of Christ forces us to do that. This is the conclusion that we've come to:[133]

One has died as the representative of all,
　　so all have died.

94

And he has died for all,
   so that those who now live, no longer live for themselves,
   but for the one who has died for them and has been raised.

So from now on we know no one 'in a worldly fashion'.
   Even if we have known Christ in a worldly way,
   we no longer know him like that.[134]
For if anyone is in Christ there is a new creation.
   The old is past,
   look, something new has happened.

   All this is from God,
   who has reconciled us with himself through Christ,
   and has given us the commission of reconciliation.
Indeed, it was God who in Christ reconciled the world to itself,
   who did not charge its transgressions to it,
   and he has sent out the word of reconciliation through us.[135]

So we represent Christ as ambassadors,
   God canvasses through us.
   On behalf of Christ we ask, Be reconciled with God.
He made to be sin the one who knew no sin,
representatively for us
   that we might become the righteousness of God in him.

So as his fellow workers we too now appeal to you,
   that you have not received the grace of God in vain;
for he says:

'at the time of salvation I have heard you,
   on the day of deliverance I have helped you.'
Look, now is the time of salvation. Look, now is the day of
   deliverance!

We're not giving anyone the slightest occasion to take offence at
us, so that our commission isn't discredited. No, in every respect
we show ourselves to be God's representatives, with stubborn
endurance:

   under pressure, in hardships, in anxieties,
   in blows, in prison, in riots,
   in labours, in watching, in hunger,

in clarity, in knowledge,
in forbearance, in friendship,
in the Holy Spirit, in sincere love,
in speaking the truth, in the power of God,

by the weapons of righteousness
armed and protected,[136]
in splendour and in shame,
in slander and approval,

as deceivers and yet true,
as misunderstood and yet understanding,
as dying and look, we live,
as hurt but not to be killed,
as insulted but always full of joy,
as poor beggars who make many rich,
as those with nothing who possess all things.[137]

O you Corinthians, I've opened my mouth to you; my heart has gone out to you. I'm not narrow. You're the ones who are narrow. Come to meet me as I come to meet you – I'm talking to you as mine, those who are descended from me[138] – and be open! Give me room among you! I've done no one an injustice, ruined no one, not gone on at anyone. I'm not saying that as a reproach. As I've said, you're in my heart, you die with me, live with me. I'm speaking to you with great openness. I'm speaking of you with great pride. I'm filled with comfort, and in all that oppresses me I'm still seized with unbounded joy.[139]

Timothy sends his greetings. You gave him a friendly welcome and set him on his way. That did him good, and I thank God that he's with me again. All my colleagues greet you, and also the other brothers and sisters who are with me.

   Greet one another with the holy kiss.

   May the Lord make his face shine upon you and be gracious to you.

The assembled church in Corinth

to

Paul, still in Ephesus

The power of the spirit be with you, and the splendour of Christ shine upon you.
Your letter has just been read out to us, and all of us gathered here are replying, openly and bluntly, as you claim you're doing.

None of us denies that your letter contains valuable passages. No one has failed to be impressed by the reading of your powerful description of the splendour of God, as you write, which marks out your commission. But it can't escape any reasonable person that you're using these great words to put down our experience of God. And with all due respect, here we have to defend ourselves.

Do you want to spoil everything for us? Tear down everything that uplifts us and supports us? Do you want to belittle us and intimidate us like children, and threaten us again with the whip again? We're no longer the dumb little ones whom you can feed with baby milk. Don't you understand? We've experienced that we're capable of the full maturity of the Spirit, God be praised. We didn't learn it from you but from the brothers whom you accuse of wanting to peddle the word of God like shabby market vendors.

Listen and understand: your attacks on our life of faith in part seem to us so nonsensical that we can only suppose that there are tragic misunderstandings or wicked slanders behind them. Or did you really mean them as they sound to us? What made you think that with Moses only the letter is important for us? It's the spirit that we're experiencing tangibly. How can you credit Moses with a 'commission of death'? Or a 'commission of condemnation'? We feel free and alive as never before. And what spirit has driven you to slander Moses as a cheat, who covers his face to disguise the fading of the divine splendour? You're turning history upside down. Why? We tell you, you're not concerned about Moses. You've aimed this humiliating sermon at us, you want to apply it to all of us, and with us to the apostles to whom we owe everything, who led us to the summit of divine light as you couldn't.

We understand your message very well, though it's incomprehensible why you should be writing it to us. The splendour passes – that's what you want to persuade us of. It doesn't last; it will fade away like a starburst. It may be that *your* splendour is fading, but ours isn't. It may be that *you* need a covering to hide the fact that your face has gone dull and your figure lacklustre. We feel God, we experience him every day. You can prophesy disaster as much as you want, you'll see. We shall progress from light to light, and no one can stop us. And if you can't understand, then come here and let us take you with us to the open heaven. Get to know the fullness of light. Or show us that Christ is working through you as powerfully as those whom you attack.

You shouldn't think that they persuaded us to write this to you. They don't persuade anyone. They don't order anything. They give us a completely free hand. They encourage us only to speak the truth. And if we're defending them, it's simply for the sake of the truth and on our own initiative. You don't know them, Paul. If you could experience them just once, you'd confess gratefully and humbly, 'Yes, they're greater than I am'. They bring the fullness. You'd stop sniping at Moses. At Moses in particular, the man of God, the enlightened one, the leader of Israel. Do you want to disqualify all Israel? Didn't you yourself teach us that Christ is the seed of Abraham?[140] They are, too: true Israelites, Hebrews,[141] ambassadors of God like Moses, commissioned by Christ, through whom Christ speaks: audible, tangible, visible. No proof is needed. It's obvious.

It's also obvious that your gospel doesn't have the same overpowering effect as theirs. You concede it yourself: your work is wearing you down, you're tormented by anxieties; you carry dying around with you, an apostle full of scrapes and bruises, a fragile container. What you write is true. Who's surprised that many scent the smell of death, the foul breath of corruption, and turn away. You're stuck in the transitory, in the morass of this world. We've risen above it, we've already forgotten the morass, left the world behind us, below us. You won't seduce us back there again. Don't try. Why should we be bothered with the world? Heaven is open.

Do you still plan to visit us? We didn't find any indication of that in your letter. What are your travelling plans? You're welcome here, you should know that. Even the apostles wouldn't object to meeting you. Perhaps one can learn from the other. Perhaps you can clear up some misunderstandings. Perhaps we've misunderstood you, and now you'll reveal the power that so far you've hidden for us. Don't you assure us that you looked Christ in the face when the divine splendour shone round him? Aren't you called to make this radiant light accessible to everyone? That's what we read in your letter. So come among us. Don't just write, show yourself!

The church greets you in great solidarity,

We all wish you peace.

Deborah the musician

to

Paul the brother

You'll understand me, even if I write rubbish, since my ears are ringing. Listen, Paul, I can't take it any more. I don't know how it's happened, but I simply can't take the way they celebrate worship any more. Inside me, do you understand? Outwardly, I'm still there. But inside me – the seductive, excitable voices of these preachers, the buzzing, swelling harmony of the ecstatic mob – I don't want to speak ill of it, but you must see that it makes me sick. It's nauseating. I want to get up, shout some obscenity, and run away. I force myself to keep quiet with all my might. That would be the end! No one would forgive me for running off shouting at a holy time.

It's nothing to do with not being allowed to play any more. The new musicians are really good, no comparison with an amateur like me. Of course I envy them. But to be honest, I could wrap their double flutes round their necks. See how I'm getting angry again. That's what the sound of their music does to me. I only have to think about it. That's what comes over me when the brothers and sisters start to preach in ecstasy. My whole being rebels.

To begin with, it was still all right. And damn it, I did try. I tried with all my might to produce in myself this overflowing Jesus happiness that everyone felt. After all, I love him. My God, Paul, believe me, I love Jesus. I want to love him. But when they all float up into higher spheres, it gets to me. Blasphemous words run through my head, really filthy ones. Excuse me. The holier everyone feels, the more ordinary I get. I keep my mouth shut.

I'm the only one who reacts in such an abnormal way. For a long time I haven't dared to write this to you. But your letter gave me some courage, You wrote that you too have your ecstasies, but for us you prefer to keep your feet on the ground. Because the love of Christ forces you. If only I could believe that! Before these people came, it was enough for me to belong to Christ. And I didn't have to generate his love. It did me good. I simply enjoyed it. Much too simply, I now learn. There's something more, bigger, more exalted, more powerful. And everyone ascends to blessed harmony with Christ. Except me. I'm dropping out. In my soul I'm 'worldly', as they put it. I'm hiding myself behind an angelic mask, but inside the devils are raging.

O my Paul, don't forget me in your prayers!

Shalom!

And come soon!

Oknos, the cook, member of the church in Corinth,

to

Paul

Things are bad with me. And I can't talk to anyone here. Tomorrow one of our guests in the tavern is travelling to Cyprus. He's going via Ephesus. I hope he'll deliver the letter. I've paid him enough. So I'm writing to you.

I've done it again, asked awkward questions in the church.

Why always these people? Others also have something to say. And everyone used to be able to have their say, as in a real democratic assembly. After all, isn't that what we are, a democratic assembly[142] round Christ?

They didn't like the grousing. Now they're cutting me. I can tell you, that's bad. You're still sitting there, but – how can I put it? – as though you were exposed in the middle of a crowd. You want to belong, join in – nothing. You don't get even a tiff. You could as well be thin air.

I've often made myself unpopular. You'll remember the dispute with Titius Justus over the money, when I took him to court before the pagan judge. You were pretty hard on me then, I must say. Your letter was a real telling off. I didn't like it at all. But it helped. We didn't have to go to the judge. Leah and Krispos between them helped us; everything was cleared up, and we're friends. You banged on the table and frightened us. It was necessary, and a good thing. Also in the business over sacrifices. It hit me hard, your sermon about the Israelites who almost got there – and then the idols, and there was a catastrophe. I'd already understood that, reluctantly, but the rebuke went home. And rightly. I'd taken Timon along to the banquet with the idols. Phalakros was there too, but that's no excuse. Now things are going better with Timon, thank God. But look, that's how it was with you, sharp, but clear. You told me off, and I came back. It wasn't the silent way in which these people deal with you. Hints in the preaching. Prayers for fallen brothers. Not so direct, but everyone knows who they mean.

God knows, I've had enough beatings in my life. But this goes beyond them all. It's worse than having your face trodden on. You can't defend yourself, you can't improve yourself, you're left high and dry and you feel an utter pig. And then you glance round at the others, but they all look away. No one will even insult you. Perhaps they'd like to; they certainly used to, but no one dares. People can't open their mouths here any more. Except to praise the good deeds of the apostles. Is that the church of Christ? Where everyone is as miserable as a dog and no one is cheerful?

I don't know why I'm writing this to you, Paul. I'd rather have had a good row with you than suffer these people who strangle your very soul.

Phrygis, the hairdresser's assistant

writes to

Paul

> See me dancing, brother!
> If I fall, what will become of me?
>
> I dance over the deep, I hover,
> all the heaviness falls away,
> everything earthly fades.
>
> My joints like water,
> my limbs burning flames,
> my back a breath.
>
> Woe to me if I don't dance!
> Look, big brother, I still keep going.
> The universe is breaking into pieces,
> I'm hovering,
> up in the dizzy heights,
> the radiant Christ.
> Keep dancing! Keep dancing! Don't stop! Don't rest!
>
> Can you see me, Paul?
> I feel that you're coming and everything is breaking up.
> Everything is falling apart and you're coming.
>
> Can you catch me if I fall?
> Can you hold the abyss together with your arms?
>
> Come quickly! Put an end to it!

Chloe and five trustworthy brothers and sisters who feel responsible for the church: Stephanas and Krispos, Chrysallis and Leah, and Erastos

to

Paul

The grace of Christ be with you.

So you came to us at a time when people had given up expecting you: you had led us to believe it would be at Pentecost, and now it's high summer. You came by ship. Didn't you really want to go by the land route, through Macedonia? We would have discovered in good time that you were on the way, and could have prepared for you. But you landed in Kenchreai, unexpected and unannounced. And your visit was a fiasco. You yourself probably felt that most clearly.

People already got annoyed when you lodged away from the central point where the church meets: not in Gaius' villa, where the church puts up its guests of honour and where everyone gathers. No, you rented a room for yourself with Krispos; you paid in advance, as if Krispos wouldn't have loved to have you as his guest. Not to mention Gaius and all of us. It's all very well, we know that you can't accept anything. And that you don't understand how loveless that seems to us. Malicious tongues are already circulating rumours. 'His trick,' they say, 'is this demonstrative modesty. He acts as someone who has no needs, but he takes money out of your purses behind your back. He even scorns your hospitality, but he takes it from you through his minions.'

Let's leave aside the gossip. There's something worse. Your quality as an apostle is at stake, and with it the roots of our church. Your appearance was depressing. And anyone who was even a bit concerned for you had to be deeply disturbed by our experience of you that evening.

You stood there before us, short and bald, an old man,[143] and spoke to us. You were excited, and sometimes difficult to understand. Almost begging us, as though you were dependent on our kindness. At any rate, that's what it felt like. And nothing came over. Not a spark of the spirit. No attractive gospel.

You knew that we had got used to different things in the meantime. But you didn't take up the challenge. At any rate, you couldn't offer anything comparable. Nothing which could even have begun to stand comparison with the weight of their preaching. Instead of that, you appealed to our sympathy. It was painful. Almost unbearable for us. And to all those to whom you weren't important, it was ridiculous. You made yourself a fool in front of them.

It's only logical that the apostles should now dismiss you as a 'bungler' at speaking. Did you notice them sitting there? You didn't think them worth even a glance, and acted as though you were all by yourself with your old church. They had expected something different from your letters. Now they've plenty to mock at: 'He's full of himself at a safe distance, but here in a personal encounter he's as servile as a petitioner.'

And it's true. You didn't take things up with them. Instead, you walked straight into it. They could sit and wait until you had got yourself all mixed up because of your eagerness, or let fly at someone in the assembly.

That's what happened, and not very gently. Someone – we'd prefer not to put his name in writing; one never knows into whose hands a letter like this might get, but you know who we mean – someone couldn't bear the paralysing silence in the church any more and let fly. Flung insults in your face which finished you off. 'You've used us,' he shouted. 'Abused us for your flimsy person, for your injured self-respect. You insinuated yourself into our souls and we got taken in. Fine words about the love of God – all calculation and deceit. And godforsaken fool that I am, I believed you.'

That's what he shouted, beside himself with rage, and as you know, there was a lot more, even worse, crude stuff, ugly talk. He shouldn't have gone on like that. Nevertheless, for many of us his anger seemed to be torn from his very soul. Perhaps it was because you talked about love, in your stammering to the church. That set him off; he couldn't bear it. If only you'd developed your theological arguments; you're a master at that, and you can match them there. Perhaps. They've also got something to offer. But at least you could have competed with them. As it is, you seemed like someone begging for love – and in the presence of your challengers at that – they were only waiting for you to put your foot in it. They're making the most of your weakness: 'His courage left him as soon as he met us face to face,' they say. He probably thought he could put himself on the same level as us. Now he'll have to learn what a true apostle is made of, and that's well beyond any standard that he's used to judging by.'

The flood of insults must have hit you harder than a whiplash. Your voice failed you, you trembled all over, and the sweat of your wretchedness smelt stronger than the smell of the stable-maids and the transport workers – what filled the house was not the healthy fragrance of Christ but the stink of anxiety and tribulation. You fell to the ground. Your body convulsed with pain. Your breath got laboured, stopped, and you lay there in front of us all as though you were dead.[144]

'Look, he has a demon,' whispered one of the apostles. 'God has made him fall.'

We dragged you out, and took you to your room at Krispos'. Some of us spent the night there. You won't remember: your body was restless, but you weren't conscious. Zinga wiped the sweat from your brow. Karylla prayed constantly for you, and all of us with her. We were afraid that you'd die on us.

But then, when the new day had already dawned, you got up, looked round in confusion, hastily packed your bag, could hardly be persuaded to have anything to eat, and stormed out, running in the direction of Kenchreai in the heat of the day. We could hardly keep up with you. No one stopped you. And shortly before we gave up, stumbling along behind you, you turned round and shouted: 'You can tell them that I'll be back. And then I won't spare anyone, anyone at all!' We stood there looking at you, saw you rushing down the long dusty road to Kenchreai. It truly was a shabby farewell. Not the right kind for brothers and sisters.

Why are we telling you all this?

For two reasons. First, we don't like the way in which the climate has changed in the church since your appearance. The apostles now feel victorious, and don't even have to fight. Now they're showing off at your expense. Playing off your set-back against you – and against those of us who, they think, still support you and read your letters in secret. They don't miss any opportunity of pouring scorn on you.

This is the way they talk: 'What do you make of this sorry performance? Is it a demonstration of spiritual power? Do you expect life from someone who's half dead? Do you expect to receive Christ's power from a weakling? Do you expect to achieve perfection through a bungler? So far he's been able to impress you by his letters. Yes, he intimidated you, and he'll try it again in the future – in letters, and from a safe distance. His letters seem weighty and strong, but when he's there in person he's weak and he stammers. You can all see it, it's obvious. Everything he does proves to be pitifully worldly. His gospel has failed, and he hasn't proved to you that Christ is speaking through him. There are none of the marks of an apostle. You look in vain for signs, wonders and mighty acts with him, not to mention the visions and revelations that we've shown you. All that is obvious is his weakness. Judge for yourself. He's nothing.'

That's how they talk. Since you left, their sermons have been full of comments like this. Their listeners respond with malicious laughter as well as rapt attention. You've made it easy for them. But we don't like it. We'd hoped that we could combine the riches of the new apostles with your gospel. Now it seems that there's only an either-or. You've contributed to that just as much as the others. But what's to happen? Things can't go on like this, otherwise the church will be torn apart.

Secondly, some of us clearly find the state of our church difficult to take. More and more often one hears disturbing things whispered quietly about this sister or that brother. Little Phrygis, who only recently was dancing among the assembly in blissful happiness, has sunk into a deep depression, and neither the blows of her owner nor the prayers of those who are close to her can bring her back to life. Quartus, the haulage contractor, half-killed his wife and children in a fit of frenzy. Deborah, the musician, rushes restlessly through the alleyways as though she were pursued by a demon. Our good Gaius, in whose villa the apostles are still living, is getting quieter and quieter, and at night he seems to be roaming round the entertainment quarters. Xenia increasingly often goes back home by herself and drinks.

There've always been lapses of this kind among us, but now everything is surrounded with rumour and suspicion. Nothing is brought up openly in the assembly, as used to be the case.

Mistrust is growing, and anxiety about the verdict of the apostles. 'Anyone who's weak is no use. Anyone who falls simply shows that Christ isn't in him.' The razor-sharp judgment with which the apostles appraise the quality of a person impressed us to begin with. Now doubts are arising as to whether this can be good. Not openly, but you can feel them. That spoils the atmosphere.

And on top of all this unhappiness a harsher wind is blowing from the 'high society' of the city. Time and again slaves are being maltreated and harrassed because they belong to us. And the hostilities against the Jewish brothers and sisters are increasing. Some have lost their jobs and their livelihood and are ashamed of being dependent on the richer brothers and sisters. And all this, too, is kept out, doesn't find a place in the assembly. It's all dismissed as worldly and therefore as unimportant.

All in all, things can't remain like this. In the long run the church can't take this sort of thing. So I, Chloe, asked some brothers and sisters to come here, reliable people, who can be relied on not to gossip. We talked for a long time. This letter is the result. I've the chance of getting it to Ephesus surreptitiously through my business connections.

Now listen, you must come again. Absolutely. We're taking you at your word. You told us you'd return, before you left us standing there in the road and went off without saying goodbye. That was verging on the outrageous, but we're biting back our annoyance and insist that you must come again. But you need more rest. You must gather your strength. For what we need from you is proof that Christ is speaking through you. Otherwise all those who came to the faith through you will have the ground taken from under their feet. It looks as if that's already happened to some people. If Christ isn't in you, if Christ doesn't work through you, then everything that we've received from you is deception and illusion. So summon up all your strength; come and sort out what you started.

Five years ago you came to us a first time, and it was a blessing. Now you've come again, and it was a catastrophe. So, Paul, come a third time. And Christ's blessing will come with you.

The sisters and brothers who wrote this letter with me greet you with their signatures.

Leah and Chrysallis: Don't think that we'd say Yes and Amen to all the steps you might take, simply because we're asking you for help. But let's find a better way of arguing.

Erastos: I haven't given up hope that we can still find a middle way. For you've become important to me, Paul, though I'm also enthusiastic about the new apostles. Come, and let's talk about it.

Krispos: Even if you didn't want it as a gift, I'm proud and happy that you stayed with me.

Stephanas: It all makes me infinitely sad.

I greet you with my signature, Chloe.

We can't send greetings from the other brothers and sisters. They don't know that we're writing to you. And please don't mention it if you write to the church. I've only told those of my own people who are taking care of the letter for me.

Peace be with you!

Paul, called to be an apostle, destined by God to bring the gospel of Jesus Christ, and all the brothers and sisters here with me

to

the church in Corinth

Grace to you and peace from God our Father and the Lord Jesus Christ, who humiliated himself for our sake and exposed himself to our enmity, even to death on the cross, to redeem us from nothingness according to the will of God our Father. To him who calls the dead to life alone belongs honour and glory for ever, Amen.[145]

I, Paul, myself beg you, by the loving friendship of Christ, I, Paul, who am 'servile in personal encounters but full of myself from a distance'. Please excuse me if I don't show off in your presence with my 'assurance'. I suspect that in that way I shall be able to cope with certain people who 'regard everything that we do as worldly'. Of course we live in worldly circumstances, but we aren't carrying on our campaign in a worldly way, for the weapons with which we fight aren't worldly, but have power from God to destroy fortresses, to bring arguments crashing down, everything that towers to heaven and opposes the knowledge of God, and to take all thought prisoner, making it obedient to Christ. And we're ready to lay down the law against all disobedience, once your obedience is restored.

Look at what's 'obvious'. If anyone is so certain that he belongs to Christ, he should also be clear that just as he himself belongs to Christ, so do we. For even if I emphasize the authority that the Lord has given us a bit too much – to build you up, not to tear you down – I won't make myself ridiculous by it.

No, I really don't want to give you the impression that I'm seeking to intimidate you with my letters. Because people say, 'His letters seem weighty and strong, but when he's there in person he's weak and he stammers.' Anyone who says this must realize that when we're present we shall act just as we say in our letters from afar.

However, we don't dare to identify or even compare ourselves with some people who commend themselves. Certainly not; they only measure themselves by themselves and compare themselves with themselves. They don't understand anything. We won't claim a competence which is 'beyond all standards', but only the standard which God has given us as the standard for our sphere of work,[146] namely to reach you too. In the end we mustn't make ourselves bigger than we are, as people who haven't lost anything with you.[147] We did in fact arrive among you with the gospel of Christ, and we don't adorn ourselves excessively with other people's pens, with other people's words. However, our hope is that when your faith grows, we shall have an even greater presence, that we shall bring the gospel to areas much further afield, which is the nature of our work. And in so doing we shall not adorn ourselves with anything that others have already done in their sphere of work.

'Let him who boasts, boast in the Lord!'

For it isn't the one who commends himself who proves to be fit, but the one whom the Lord commends.

If only you could have taken a bit of unreasonableness from me! After all, you used to be able to take it from me. After all, I'm fighting over you with a divine passion. I've finally betrothed you to a husband, to Christ, to bring him a wife who belongs to him alone. My only fear is that just as the serpent led Eve astray with its deception, so your thoughts could be corrupted, away from the clear, untroubled love of Christ. For if someone comes and preaches a different Jesus from the one we preached, or if you receive another spirit which you didn't receive before, or another gospel than the one that you accepted, then you're taking it remarkably!

In my view, at any rate, I don't fall short of these super-apostles in any way. Though I may be a 'bungler' as far as speaking is concerned, I'm not in knowledge. I've made that clear to you all on every occasion. Or did I commit a sin in belittling myself to make you great, because I handed on the gospel of God to you without charge? I've fleeced other communities: that's where I got the money for my commission among you. When I was with you, even in the greatest need I wasn't a burden on anyone. For if I lacked anything, the brothers and sisters who came from Macedonia helped me. I was determined not to be a burden on you in any way, and my determination will continue. By the truth of Christ which is in me, all those in the region of Achaia can sing my praises, and no one will make them keep quiet? Why? Because I don't love you? God knows I do!

But I shall go on doing what I'm doing, in order to destroy the case of those who would like to have a case against me, so as to stand on the same basis as me with their self-glorification. For these people are pseudo-apostles,[148] deceitful workers, who disguise themselves as apostles of Christ. That's not surprising: even Satan disguises himself as an angel of light. So it's hardly a great surprise if those who receive his commission also disguise themselves as people with a commission of righteousness. Their end will match their deeds.

Once again, let no one take me for a fool. But if you do, at least take me for a fool so that I can praise myself a little. What I'm now saying is not in the Lord's sense, but as though I were surrounded by nonsense, in this situation in which only impressions count. Since many people are praising themselves in a very worldly way, I shall praise myself too. Intelligent as you are, you do bear fools gladly. Indeed you take it when people put chains on you, snatch things from you, take advantage of you, set themselves above you, strike you in the face. To my shame, I must say that we were too weak for that.

But whatever anyone brings out to show his courage – I'm talking nonsense – I can match him. Are they Hebrews? So am I. Are they Israelites? So am I. Are they the seed of Abraham? So am I. Do they have a commission from Christ? Now I'm talking quite crazily. I have a far better one. I'm way beyond them in being battered, way beyond them in being imprisoned, way beyond them in beatings, in danger of death time and again. I've had the forty strokes less one five times from the Jews, and the Roman kind of beating[149] three times; I've been stoned once, suffered shipwreck three times, spent a night and a day on the open sea. I've often been on the road, in danger from floods, in danger from attacks, in danger from my own people, in danger from Gentiles, in danger in the city, in danger in the wilderness, in danger on the sea, in danger from pseudo-brothers.[150] Plenty of toil and plenty of trials, often without sleep, hungry and thirsty, often without food, cold and exposed – quite apart from the daily pressure on me of my anxiety for all the churches. Who is weak, and I'm not weak? Who falls and I don't get angry?

If there has to be some showing off, then I shall show off the things that demonstrate my weakness. God, the Father of the Lord Jesus, praise be to him for ever, knows that I'm not lying. In Damascus, the governor of king Aretas had the city of the Damascenes watched in order to catch me, and I was lowered down the walls from a window in a basket – that's the only way I could escape him.

There has to be some showing off. There's nothing to be gained by it, but I want to go on to talk about 'visions and revelations' of the Lord. I know of a man in Christ: fourteen years ago – whether in the body, I don't know, or outside the body; I don't know, but God does – this man was caught up into the third heaven. And I know that this man – whether in the body or without the body, I don't know, but God knows – was caught up into paradise and heard unutterable words which no human being can speak.

I want to show off for this man. But I don't want to show off for myself, except with my weaknesses. Anyway, if I wanted to show off, I wouldn't be a fool, since I would be speaking the truth. But I'd prefer not to, so that no one may attribute to me more than he sees in me or hears of me, because of the extraordinary revelations.

So to keep me from getting above myself, a thorn has been put in my flesh, an angel of Satan, to afflict me,[151] so that I don't get above myself. Three times I've prayed to the Lord to remove it from me. And he's told me:

'You have enough, my grace;
for power is made real in weakness.'

Thus I prefer to show off over my weaknesses, so that the power of Christ enters into me. That's why I affirm what makes me weak – insult, hardships, persecutions and anxieties – in the light of Christ: for when I'm weak, then I'm strong.

I've become a fool. You forced me to it. I really didn't need to be commended by you. For I'm not at all inferior to these 'super-apostles', even if I'm 'nothing'. The marks shown by the apostles were untiringly performed among you through signs, miracles and mighty acts.[152] In what did you fall short of the other churches, except that I myself wasn't a burden on you? Forgive me this wrong.

Look, I'm ready to come to you a third time, and this time again I won't be a burden on you; I'm not looking for what you have, but for you. Children don't need to pay for their parents, but parents for their children. I will gladly spend, indeed be completely spent, for you. If I love you more and more, am I to be loved all the less?

Let's leave it at that: I myself wasn't a burden on you. But, crafty as I am, I 'took money from your purses behind your backs'. Did I perhaps 'fleece' you with the help of one of those I sent to you? For example, I gave Titus a commission, and sent brother Tychikos[153] with him. Did Titus take anything from you? Didn't we go our way with the same attitude? Indeed, didn't we take the same steps?

You probably thought long ago that we would defend ourselves to you. We're standing in the sight of God. We speak before him, in Christ. And of course, beloved ones, so that you will be built up again. For I'm afraid that when I come I may not find you as I'd like you to be, and that then you won't find me as you'd like me to be either; that perhaps there will be disputes, jealousy and angry outbursts, intrigues, gossip and scheming, conceit and chaos. I'm afraid that when I come again my God my once again humble me before you, and that I may have to lament over many who haven't turned from the former shameful deeds that they've done, from the filth and the fornication and the addictions.

So I'm coming to you a third time. 'Any matter must be confirmed by the evidence of two or three witnesses.' I announced on my second visit and now announce again in my absence to those who transgressed before, and also to everyone else: when I come again, I won't spare them — as you want evidence that Christ is speaking through me. He isn't weak in dealing with you, but is powerfully at work among you. For he was crucified in weakness, but lives by the power of God. So we too are weak in him, but we shall live him by the power of God, and with you. Examine yourselves to see whether you're in the faith, test yourselves. Don't you notice anything of Jesus Christ at work in you? If you don't, you must have become suddenly quite useless. But I hope you'll see that we aren't useless.

We pray to God that you don't do anything wrong. We're not concerned that our criticism[154] should be proved right. We prefer to stand as incompetent critics, and for you to be doing good. For we can't do anything against the truth, but only for the truth. We rejoice if we're weak and you are strong. What we pray for is for you to be restored. That's why I'm writing this to you from afar, so that when I come I don't deal too harshly with you; for the Lord has given me my authority to build up, and not to tear down.

Otherwise, brothers and sisters, rejoice, allow yourselves to be restored, accept criticism, pull together, keep the peace, and the God of love and peace will be with you. Greet one another with the holy kiss. All the saints greet you.

The grace of our Lord Jesus Christ and the love of God and the felllowship of the Holy Spirit be with you all!

The church of Jesus Christ in Corinth, Achaia

to

Paul, the apostle of God

The loving friendship of our God be with you.

It's over. Thank God, it's over. Only now, when you shook us awake so powerfully, did we recognize the extent of the misery, did we sense the terror at being scattered, far from the summits of divine enthusiasm, naked and lost, out of the reach of the loving voice of the Father.

You woke us up, dear, dear Paul, with your rough letter – but perhaps even more through Titus, whom you sent to us with the letter and who helped us in our confusion. We're deeply grateful to him. He's become a true friend to us. He brought us not only your letter but the effective grace of God himself. So we kept him longer with us than was originally planned, and even now it's painful to part with him.

Perhaps we couldn't have borne your letter without Titus. It hit us hard. It was the truth that hit us. You didn't try to fool us, took no account of our sensibilities. Many of us were insulted and furious when Titus read the letter out the first time. Nothing can be more intolerable than the truth. But you didn't spare yourself anything either. Behind the biting irony we could sense clearly your desperate passion. Perhaps it was this that touched us all in our hidden misery.

It wasn't at all certain how things would go. Our 'great masters' still sat there and used every opportunity to blunt your words: 'Can't you read between the lines?' they called out. 'Don't you understand that he means something quite different from what he's writing? That he's abusing us as tyrants, simply so that he can lord it over your faith? Surely you're not confusing this double-tongued worldly cleverness with divine wisdom? Look how confused the man's plans are: first he promises to come on foot via Macedonia; then he suddenly lands by ship; then he threatens to come again without delay – but look, now he's giving himself time and coming through Macedonia. Instead, once again he sends you a substitute and a grim letter. He says "Yes, yes" and means "No". He says "No, no" and means "Yes". We call that a worldly kind of plan! How is one to awaken any trust in the announcements of God if one can't even rely on his own announcements? If he lightly makes promises and doesn't keep them? Does that look like the assurance that he claims? You ought to be ashamed of such an apostle!' They staked everything on showing that you were unreliable and we were your credulous prey, and they probably hoped to strike an echo in the one who was so poisonous to you on your visit, and the many who had quietly felt as he did.

Titus let them speak, them and everyone who wanted to say a word. And with God's help, he succeeded in rekindling the spirit of prophetic controversy: experience was set against experience, interpretation against interpretation. Paralysed tongues produced clear words; thoughts which had been buried and kept down forced their way into the light, contradictory, passionate, alive. The spell of enforced agreement over piety broke, the tyranny of solidarity without grace crumbled. And that visibly irritated those who had been leaders hitherto. That's probably why they went on making these cheap objections, which were really beneath them.

The argument came to a head when the talk got round to the insults that you'd suffered and the one of our number who had screamed his hatred in your face. For a long time it wasn't clear where this would lead, since even when the 'apostles' wanted to egg him on to support them, he sat there dumb and didn't utter a sound. Then Stephanas stood up, asked for quiet, and said in a firm voice: 'I think that this is a matter between us and this brother. We should discuss it without visitors.'

The 'visitors' didn't wait to see what the church decided. They felt that now they wouldn't get a majority against Stephanas. But before they went off, they stood in front of the one who had insulted you, looked at him for a long time, and finally asked, 'Do you want to come with us?' The person concerned got up, looked them in the face, and said 'No.' Then they disappeared. We could begin to deal with that shameful attack on you.

The discussion wasn't easy. It became clear to us that the person concerned wasn't the only one on trial, but that we were all accused with him. We had allowed you to be brutally slandered. No one had done anything to stop it. Chloe even conceded that partly, at any rate, at the time he had spoken to her from the soul, and a number of people could confirm that. But Boaz said that we shouldn't act as though nothing had happened. Precisely because so far we hadn't distanced ourselves from the perpetrator, we now had to give a clear sign. This was finally approved by the majority. We agreed that for a certain period we should treat the person concerned as a pagan or an unbeliever. He accepted the verdict and went silently from our midst. Since then he's come to the assemblies and sat right at the back, on the visitor's bench, alongside a gaunt, one-eyed Cretan, who has been sitting there for months and can't decide whether to come to baptism.

Now it's become inevitable that our friend and brother Titus has to leave us, and we're celebrating the supper with him for the last time. We would so like to keep him with us, since he really was like an angel of God to us. But the bad news from Asia disturbed him and us very much, and we understand that he's eager to leave and travel to you – though no one knows whether he will meet you in Troas, as agreed, or in Ephesus, or indeed whether he will ever see you again. The last news we had was three days ago, from brothers who were travelling through, and what they reported caused us great anxiety. First of all we'd heard only that you and two other colleagues from Ephesus had been arrested, but it seemed to us more like being held for questioning, and they also said that you were in good shape and could keep in touch with the brothers and sisters.[155] Titus thought that he could now allow himself time, since he was to have met you in Troas, and in any case that would be possible only after you'd been released. Of course that was fine by us: we didn't know how your trial was developing. Now we hear that things aren't going at all well with you or with the others, and that some influential people are doing all they can to eliminate you and destroy the churches in Asia. We're anxious for you. We keep pestering God in our prayers for you and the two people who are in prison with you, and for all the brothers and sisters in Ephesus. At the moment we don't even know whether you're alive. The uncertainty has paralysed us these last days. But Leah took our depression away with her prophetic clairvoyance. 'Do what has to be done,' she cried out to us. 'No matter what, our letter will help Paul, whether in Macedonia or in Troas, in prison in Ephesus or before the judgment seat of God.'

So we got down to preparing Titus for the journey. And today we're celebrating the supper with him for the last time, knowing that the cup of the new covenant also unites us with you, wherever you are, in prison or in freedom or already wholly with Christ. Chrysallis strikes up her new song, and we all sing it with her.

Mystery of God
greater than all
that men can devise.
Into our darkness
down he comes
Lord of all light.

Reconciles our world
makes strangers friends
enduring death;
where the mighty pass judgment,
robbers beside him,
God crowns his Son.

There, from the depth
of earthly confusion,
you look upon us.
God, you are love,
greater than all
that men devise.

And Phrygis takes up Chrysallis' song, and her voice echoes the depression she suffered :

Weary to death,
from high in the clouds,
I fell to the ground.

Heavily I landed,
look they are there,
the arms of God.

They hold me fast.
Everything hurts,
Jesus, I live!

Deborah accompanies the song on her instrument, and it sounds as if her flute is laughing for joy. Never have we heard such music.

Now we've eaten the bread of reconciliation and drunk from the cup of blessing. and many people want to send greetings and tell you personally things they've long kept quite about. We often talk like this after the supper: say what has happened, share with one another what has changed, thank God.

Esther
We were terrified, Mattat and I. We wanted to belong to Christ. That's all we wanted, nothing else. So we looked for marks to indicate who really belonged to Christ. And suddenly we were denying that you and others belonged to Christ. We were terrified when we understood that. I think that there's only one distinguishing mark for belonging to Christ: Christ himself as he died on the cross.

Krispos
I now know how they caught me: strict leadership, a clear line, everyone in agreement. Before that, everyone was often at cross-purposes and the to-ing and fro-ing always confused me. Even now, I wonder about the future. How can we ensure the unity of the church? And also the unity of the whole world-wide church? At any rate I've recognized that it can't be like that. The spirit of Christ has nothing to do with forcing people.

Phalakros
I've become clear about many things. Above all I didn't want to be guilty. It couldn't be true that I'd ruined poor Timon's health and work, his whole life, and Rufina's as well, simply by being frivolous and showing off. Better get intoxicated. Especially if it was the intoxication of Christ. It was terribly hard to grasp that. Timon himself has helped me here. Now both of us have talked to each other about it a lot. And Titus. He's good! He doesn't let you take off. Or himself either. He just keeps sitting by you, when

you're there in the filth. Shows you the filth that you're sitting in. It's as if Christ himself had landed in the midst of it, right next to you. And you can confess, 'Yes, it's my filth. That was me. Thank God the pressure's finished.'

Mara
I can't tell you how glad I am that the ghastly charade is over. I was never one of the enthusiasts; that sort of thing simply doesn't turn me on, you see. All this unearthly stuff made me sick from the start. And I felt bad that I'd stopped complaining about it so soon. I tried once, but just didn't get anywhere. It was like hitting a pile of cotton wool. Probably I didn't find the right tone to be taken seriously. So I just put my head down and let the sounds go over me. And I do feel bad that I gave up so quickly. You didn't give up, Paul, though they played such dirty tricks on you, and I'm grateful for that. You didn't give us up, but rather let yourselves be provoked beyond bearing, just as Christ himself didn't give us up. Thank you, Paul! And thank you, Christ!

Boaz
I've learned that Jesus is more than Paul. And more than Cephas, and Apollos, and anyone else who presents himself as an apostle.

Titius Justus
I have to confess that I suspected you: I believed that rumour about shady dealings with money. And I passed it on. When people said, 'Surely not, at least not Paul', I shook my head and said, 'Who knows?' Your behaviour did in fact seem strange to me: you collected enormous sums for Jerusalem and won't accept even a bowl of soup. I still don't understand it. I learned from the Jews to give alms and do good. Completely without respect of persons. Why not for you? Anyway, excuse my mistrust. And my malicious talk.

Quartus
I maltreated my children and harmed my wife. I still want to creep away for shame. I can't say more.

Fortunatus

I was disappointed in you. When we visited you in Ephesus your work seemed to me to be laborious, meagre and not very effective. I thought that it must be possible to get more impressive results with new figures, that there was a need for young workers who weren't worn out, with bright ideas. And when we returned to Corinth, there they were, these young, dynamic power-houses. As if to order.

Erastos

With some pain I've distanced myself from this way of enthusing the mass of people. Certainly these incorruptible leaders fascinated me. They played on our longings like musical instruments. They were able to silence all the dissonance and bring everyone into harmony for the great goal: to experience as they did, to desire as they did, to be as they were. The power that they had over us stirred me like a fever. Power over our feelings and desires and wills. To gather masses like this and lead them to a tremendous goal. To unite different kinds of men and women and peoples, to sweep them together into a gigantic kingdom which no one could resist any longer.

Now that it's over I recognize my political desires, I know that that's how I wanted to influence people. As powerfully as they did. To have the masses entranced at my feet.

When you lay there on the floor, trembling, deeply wounded by the mob, by us, I saw a sacrifice in front of me. I began to understand what such power does. I resisted, struggled: what can I rescue of my political plans? And what can rescue me from my political megalomania?

Now I feel devastated. I'm not yet sure what to do. Perhaps I'll withdraw my candidacy in the city elections.[156] There are already far too many leaders on the political stage who enthuse the people in order to bend them to their own interests. And I though that this was a way of helping Christ to victory.

Hannah

I just want to report that Fortunatus and I got married, that I'm pregnant and indescribably happy. Fortunatus can't stop talking about it. I know that there are more important things, and that you won't jump for joy as soon as you hear it. Still, we did it. In God's name. And Christ will bless us.

Gaius

I'm thinking about what it means for rich people to belong to Christ. I have the villa. Everyone meets here with me. The guests of the church stay with me. And those gentlemen were my guests. Clearly, for a householder, to belong to Christ means to be a good host. I'm glad to do this. My house and my business are at everyone's disposal. And I don't make much fuss about it. But I sat there being a hospitable brother and heard their poisonous talk. How they made some of us think bad thoughts. I encouraged them to get on with it and tuck in. That was all. I could have thrown them out. After all, it's my house. No one else can show them out, only me. I didn't. I remained a good host. I was very impressed by your recommendation, Paul, to live in the world as if one had nothing to do with it. I was well off, and acted as though my riches weren't my concern. And it was also a bit painful to be richer than all the other brothers and sisters, but acting as though one had no power. So I've been avoiding my responsibilities, letting bad things happen when I could have intervened. Because I'm the householder and have the right, and no one else does. And because Christ evidently entrusted me with my property. That I have space where everyone can meet is part of the commission for which I must be responsible.

I still don't know how things will work out – what is practicable, I mean. But it's become clear to me that that's the only way.

Melas

My theological thinking has had some gaps torn in it. It's no longer all of a piece. That's a good thing. Hitherto it was all too coherent. The conflicts which broke out are too big for it to be possible to hold them together logically. At first I thought that it was bad to have differences of opinion, to have different accents in any kind of theology. But then we all learned – and I can't cope with this purely intellectually – that the issue was existence: your existence, and the existence of all of us as those who belong to Christ.

At present I'm trying to work out whether this gap has made

my previous theological approach completely unusable, or whether the truth which I've just understood with your help can't also be expressed evocatively, and in a way which is understandable to educated Jews and Greeks, by the methods of Egyptian learning. It's clear to me that such an attempt won't work out without paradoxes. But why shouldn't such paradoxes be more expressive than smooth truths? What you said in your letter about the nonsense of God which surpasses human wisdom has become important to me in this connection. I'm thinking along the following lines: Christ as the embodiment of divine wisdom, who was already with God when he created the world, through whom so to speak everything was created – a theologically educated Jew, or a Greek interested in philosophy, could understand the unique significance of Christ in this way. And then would come the unthinkable, unutterable break: this divine Christ becomes flesh, enters the world – nonsense to any thinking person. But God's love for the world surpasses all that we can think. I myself keep being constantly amazed at it all over again. It had never really become clear to me until you wrote to us, that God is reconciling the world, the cosmos, our whole rotten society, with himself. – I'm going on too long. I hope that we'll find time to talk about this when you're with us.

Xenia
I've done a lot and said a lot I'm ashamed of. I just want to keep quiet for a while and think.

I too, Tertius, confess that the events which are behind us have shaken and moved me, even if my feelings have tended to lie hidden behind the usual objectivity of a secretary and scribe. Deep in my soul I hate disputes and quarrelling. Or to be more precise, they make me anxious. I've come off worst in them too often. Sometimes it seems that the spirit of Christ reaches a goal through the midst of threatening battles. This experience will make me think for a long time.

Now Titus will set off for Macedonia, visit the churches and then travel on to Troas, and if necessary to Ephesus. We're giving him this letter which is as important for us as it is for you, and we hope that Titus can deliver it to you, wherever you are.

God protect you and free you from the power of men, you and all those who are in prison with you.

Paul, an apostle of Christ by God's resolve, and Timothy the brother

to

the church of God in Corinth and to all the saints in the whole of Achaia

Grace to you and peace from God our Father and the Lord Jesus Christ.

Blessed be God, the Father of our Lord Jesus Christ, the Father of mercy and God of all comfort, who comforts us in all our torment, so that we can comfort others in all that torments them, through the comfort which we ourselves receive from God. For just as abundantly as the sufferings of Christ come upon us, so abundantly we also find comfort through Christ. And in the end both are in your service: if we suffer torment, it is because we are concerned with your comfort and your salvation; and if we are comforted, it is because you too are experiencing comfort and as a result getting the power to withstand the same suffering, which you suffer as well as we do. And as our hope for you is strong, we know that you are bound to us not only by the suffering but also by the comfort.

For we don't want to conceal from you, brothers and sisters, the torments we experienced in Asia: we were burdened far beyond our powers, so that we even despaired of life. Indeed, in our minds we had already accepted the death sentence. That was so as not to rely on ourselves, but on God who raises the dead. He has delivered us from this deadly peril and he will deliver us. We've pinned our hopes on him; he will also deliver us in the future. You're all helping us here because you're praying for us – and many others will also be giving thanks for us, many voices giving thanks for the help that we've experienced.

What we are proud of – and our consciences are witnesses – is this. We've acted in the world with the blunt clarity of God: in other words, not with 'worldly cleverness' but by the power of the grace of God – and especially with you. We're writing you nothing but what you can read and understand, and we hope that now you will finally understand – you've already in fact partially understood – that we are your pride, just as you are ours, on the day of our Lord Jesus.

That was my 'assurance'. And therefore I planned first to come to you, so that you received God's grace from me a second time,[157] and then to go from you to Macedonia, and come back again from Macedonia to you and have you as my escort to Judaea. That's what I planned. Was that frivolous? What was there in my plans that was 'planned after the manner of the world', so that when I said 'Yes, yes', it meant 'No, no' at the same time? God is my guarantee that our word to you is not Yes and No at the same time! For the Son of God, Christ Jesus, who has been made known among you by us, by me and Silvanus and Timothy, was not Yes and No, but it was Yes through him. For all the announcements of God in him are Yes. That's why we also respond Amen through him, to the glory of God. But God himself establishes us and you in fellowship with Christ. He has anointed us and set his seal on us,[158] and as a guaranteee of life he gives us the spirit in our hearts.

I call God to witness, by my life – it was only to spare you that I didn't come back to Corinth. It wasn't a matter of 'lording it over your faith'. No, we're fellow workers in your joy. For in the faith you stand on your own feet. But that's what I firmly planned: not another visit with such hurts. For if I hurt you, who else is there who could cheer me up again? All those who could do that have been hurt by me. So I've just put all this to you in writing, so that I don't have to come again and suffer yet more hurt – from those who should have made me happy. For I can count on it that if I'm happy it makes all of you equally happy. I wrote under intolerable pressure and with much anxiety in my heart, and with many tears. Not to hurt you, but so that you could sense even more the love that I feel for you.

Now if anyone has hurt me, he's hurt not only me but all of you, or at any rate – don't let's exaggerate – part of you. This disciplining that the person concerned has been given by the majority is now enough. No, really you should now forgive him and comfort him, so that his pain isn't so bad that he drowns in it. So I beg you to confirm your love to him. That's also why I've written, to see how you're proving yourselves, whether you're completely obedient. And if you forgive anyone anything, then so do I. Indeed, if I had anything to forgive, whatever it might be, I've also forgiven it for your sake in the face of Christ. In this way we won't be distracted by Satan, since we're well aware of his plans.

You should know that when I got to Troas – I wanted to make Christ known there, and also found doors opened to me through the Lord – I was inwardly restless because I didn't find Titus my brother there. So I said good-bye to them and travelled to Macedonia. But even when we got to Macedonia we were still restless – indeed, we were under a lot of pressure: disputes outside and anxieties inside. But God who comforts the oppressed comforted us. Titus arrived. And he comforted us not only by his arrival but by the comfort which he had received from you. He told us how you longed for us, how shattered you had been, and how passionately you had devoted yourselves to me. So I became happier and happier. Therefore if I touched you on a sore point with my letter, I don't regret it. Though I'm sorry I did so, I can see that even if this letter hurt you for a moment – but now I'm glad – not, of course, that you were hurt but that the hurt changed you. For you were hurt in God's way, so that what we did caused you no harm at all. For being hurt in God's way brings a change of direction, towards salvation, and one mustn't regret that. By contrast, the hurts the world brings result in death. Look at what being hurt in God's way has brought you: power, clarity, indignation, fear, longing, resolute action and finally putting right injustice! With all this you've shown that you're clear about this matter. And that means that even if I wrote that letter to you, it wasn't really about who had done an unjustice and who had suffered an injustice, but about your devotion to us coming to light before God. That comforted us.

But the comfort wasn't all. We were quite indescribably delighted at Titus' enthusiasm. He drew inner strength from all of you. I had sometimes been enthusiastic to him about you, and you proved me right.[159] Indeed, just as we always spoke truthfully to you, so our songs of praise to Titus have also proved true. And now his feelings are quite especially with you, remembering how you all put yourselves at his disposal and how you welcomed him with evident respect. I'm so delighted that I can rely on you completely and utterly.[160]

You can see that I'm already on the way to you. I shall set off from Philippi in a few days. But I want to spend some time in Thessalonike and Beroia, since the brothers and sisters there need our help, and we need theirs. But from there we shall travel on to you without any long stops on the way. Prepare some lodgings for us, for me and my other colleagues and the delegates from the churches.

Greet one another with the holy kiss.

I greet you all, Paul.

Greetings from the whole church in Philippi.

And may the God of peace perfect you according to his will; may he preserve you unharmed, spirit and soul and body; may no accusations be made against at the coming of our Lord Jesus Christ.

The one who calls is faithful. And he will do it!

Nannos the shipbuilder in Corinth, Achaia

to

Paul, the apostle, and all the brothers and sisters in Macedonia

The friendship of God and the love of Jesus Christ be with you. First, thanks for your support. You've rescued me from the wilderness. Everyone agreed immediately and ended the temporary exclusion. As a sign of their trust they've commissioned me to write to you in the name of us all. Although I never really learned to write. I can read blueprints, and put together inventories, but I've never written a letter in my life before. However, Achaikos is helping me. And I'm glad to be writing to you.

Oh Paul, I was so glad to belong again! You put a line under everything. There is no longer any ill-feeling between us. Thank you, Paul. I'm not ashamed to write openly about it. The brothers and sisters were considerate. They didn't mention my name in their letter and you didn't in yours. Now that you've forgiven me there's no need for precautions. All the world can know it: I, Nannos, did you an injustice. You, Paul, called for reconciliation. Everyone is delivered: the old is gone – look, the new has come about. Thank God!

I can tell you that it was bad to sit out there, cut off from the fellowship of the brothers and sisters. To be cast out with all the curious and the unbelievers every time the meal began. How often I then had to go away, hungry and thirsty in body and soul. I suffered miserably. Being excluded – that's the worst of all. Especially when you really belonged the first time. And you don't know whether you should believe it, whether it's really true. I'd never experienced it; all my life I'd just stood by. The church was the miracle for me. I was one of them. Right in their midst. And then to be thrown out again, if only for a while – that was terrible.

I could have avoided it. The gentlemen who thought that they were the better apostles made me an offer. They would have taken me with them. They even tried to buy my freedom. After my attack on you they regarded me as their most loyal supporter. So, come with us, they said. It led to nothing. Not just because they couldn't have bought my freedom. The firm doesn't get rid of a specialist like me. Probably the whole firm would have had to turn to Christ first. But even if they had managed it, I wouldn't have gone with them. I was never their man. They didn't understand properly. I was near to going over to them, in revenge, to hurt you even more. But not out of conviction.

I want you to know what was going on inside me. Not as an excuse. You've forgiven me, and that's enough, I needn't hide it any more. But you must understand; it's important for me. And I think it's also important for you to understand me.

I was desperately disappointed in you, and full of irrational anger. I'd pinned everything on you, all my trust, all my love. I'd never had such expectations of anyone in my life as I had of you. You brutally shattered my hopes, trampled on my love, and exploited and abused my trust. That's what it looked like. I couldn't interpret your painful appearance in any other way, when you let these eloquent gentlemen triumph. You'd become a trapper to me, someone who ensnares souls, who doesn't do what he leads people to believe, who proclaims the Lord of all lords and then doesn't have the strength to force a couple of big mouths to their knees. And when you went on to say something about love, it sounded to me like sheer mockery. Love!

You know, I haven't much experience of love, and none at all of trust. I don't even know who put me in the world and kept me alive. Presumably someone somewhere picked me up and fed me until I was big enough to bring a few drachmas from a slave dealer. I don't remember. I found myself in the ownership of a Roman lady who used me as a cute figure to decorate her household. She called me Nannos, 'dwarf', and I was certainly tiny. The name's stuck. I never got really tall. But I'm strong. They sold me cheaply to the shipyard. I worked my way up there, from dogsbody to chief constructor. My ships sail well, I've given the firm some advantages in the market, and in this way I've a certain value. And of course my colleagues envy me. But there was no love anywhere. You had to be mistrustful; no one asked how you felt inside and it would have been very unwise to show it. At best the inner life is given a very circumscribed place in religion: duly prostrated before the gods of the powerful, one may long for mercy. But here, too, trust was inappropriate.

Until I got to know you. You and Silvanus and Timotheos and the church made up of slaves and freemen, of outsiders and notables of the city, all equally filled with the love of Christ which you depicted to us, which spoke to us from you. Friendship, not gracious condescension. Recognition, and not just to increase production. Putting people right to help them, not to humiliate then. Anyone who can do that is a master! Standing the laws of the world on their head. And what a man who represents this Lord of all lords! Superior to everyone: to the bosses in the shipyard, the priests, the scholars, the philosophers, the politicians – none of them can touch Paul. No one can do what Paul and his Christ do.

That's how I loved you, Paul. Can you understand? As the embodiment of all perfection, incomparable, unbeatable.

When those other apostles led our friends here to the summits of ecstasy, when they wanted to surpass you and made you look ridiculous, it didn't disturb me. I knew that you would come and they would cringe. You would say a word and they would confess, 'Yes, Paul is stronger than we are: his gospel outshines all our magic.' I waited a long time. But you didn't come. Kept me waiting, although I was in need; you let them make a fool of you and draw more and more brothers and sisters on to their side. In secret I cried out to God finally to bring you – things couldn't go on like that. But even God took his time. The waiting got more and more painful and the anger more and more bitter, and when you finally got there, just one thought kept hammering on my brain. Now, dear Paul, just show what you can do. It's your last chance. Win or disappear.

You lost the battle before it really began. Ingloriously and repulsively. I was the one who was bruised. The naive fool who had entrusted his innermost being to a swindler. All that was left was a devastating rage. You were on the receiving end. Even while I was ranting at you I could see, could feel, that it hit you like an axe, that you fell to the ground devastated, defenceless, unprotected. You hadn't put your armour on; the axe didn't bounce off; it struck you in the flesh. I saw it and still couldn't stop hurting you more and more. Like the mercenaries who kept on striking and trampling on Christ, driven by the hatred that had been unleashed.

They cast me out for it. Their verdict was a just one. I suffered terribly, and understood some things. I couldn't stop thinking of your letter, the one before last which Titus brought. Again I sensed how wounded you were. How my thrust hadn't rebounded from you like an iron shield. That was a new experience. It confused me and touched me strangely. I sensed something of the power which is made real in weakness. When I think back to it now, I can see how you were always talking and writing about this weakness. But I never understood it. I took the lists of all your trials and tribulations as artistic figures of speech, just as some street philosophers celebrate their superiority to pain and passion.[161] Only now has it dawned on me, in my own misery, that it's real. In you and also in Christ. Now I understand why you kept confronting us time and again with the execution of Christ. I found it quite remarkable, out there: somehow I was nearer to you than I had been inside. I found Christ, the outcast Christ; indeed I found him by my side.

I've also found a new friend: a mercenary from Crete. He only has one eye, and that always has a sceptical look. I always used to sit next to him on the visitor's bench. He sat there for months, undecided, as I once did. We get on well. When the church had me back, he also plucked up his courage and came to be baptized.

Now I've told you a lot about myself. I mustn't forget to tell you what the church commissioned me to say.

First, they're all relieved and praise God that he's kept you alive, and that you've been released from prison. I personally give special thanks to my God. If you'd left us in the midst of our quarrel, as my enemy – well, it doesn't bear thinking about. It would have been as if I'd killed you. But you're alive, thank God, you're alive!

Secondly, we all thank you for your letter from Philippi. What you wrote has happened: the comfort which you received from God has got to us. And it will go on from us to many people who need it.

Thirdly, we confirm once again that we definitely want to take part in the aid for the brothers and sisters in Jerusalem. Titus has reported to us that the churches in Asia have already collected a handsome sum, that he's now getting the gifts together in Macedonia, and making all the arrangements for handing them over. He also told us yet again at length how the whole thing began, a good seven years ago, when you were in Jerusalem with Barnabas and committed yourself to making this collection. Only then did we really become clear what significance the action had in holding the church together: the churches from the peoples of the world coming to Jerusalem and bringing their treasures to the saints of Israel! Krispos read out a passage from the scriptures to us and explained to us the proclamation of the prophet Isaiah on Jerusalem:[162]

'Then you will see,
terrified and inspired in your heart,
how there turns to you
the wealth of the sea,
the peoples and nations.
To you they will come.'

Now that will be fulfilled. Erastos said it for all of us. 'Corinth must be there,' he exclaimed, 'Corinth, the meeting point of all the peoples and nations of the earth, the trading post of all the riches of the seas. Corinth, where the ways cross from east to west and from north to south. With our great variety, aren't we a living image of the world of nations? Greeks and Romans, Arabs and Egyptians, Africans and northerners, people from all the islands and even from distant Spain are gathered together here . . .'

He would certainly have gone on talking longer, he was so enthusiastic, but Mara interrupted him affectionately in jest, 'Are you trying out your speech for the centenary already?'[163] They all laughed, and Erastos had to laugh, too. 'But it's true,' he said, 'Corinth must be there when the peoples bring their treasures.' And we all agreed about that. So we're waiting for your instructions.

My dear Paul, it's good that you're on your way to us. We don't grudge the churches in Macedonia your visit, but at the same time we hope that you'll be here soon. Make sure that you're staying with us before the winter storms. Gaius has already got a room ready for you, and there's plenty of room for all the others who are coming with you. We're so looking forward to seeing you.

Greetings to Timothy and especially our friend Titus. The brothers and sisters from Kenchreai and all the churches of Achaia send their greetings to you.

Greetings from Achaikos: I helped Nannos to write the letter.

I, Nannos, greet you with my new song. It came to me when I'd been cast out. I sang it when I was welcomed back again. They all joined in, and they all send greetings with their song:

Jesus, our friend,
you suffer our torments,
die in our misery,
wonderful Lord,
so strangely near,
brother in weakness,
power of God.

Paul and Timothy

to

the church in Corinth

Grace be with you and peace![164]
We can report to you, brothers and sisters, what God's loving concern[165] has brought about in the churches of Macedonia. Under great pressure, which they withstood, unbounded joy arose, and from the depths of their poverty a stream of sincere kindness flowed. I can testify that they gave as much as they could, indeed more than they could, quite spontanously – they formally urged us to let them take part in the relief work for the saints. They surpassed all our hopes: they gave themselves, above all to the Lord, and then, by God's will, also to us.

So we were able to commission Titus to complete this relief action which he had also begun with you; he has already set it in motion. And just as you are rich in every respect, rich in faith, in speech and in knowledge, rich in your complete commitment and rich in our love which is with you – see that you also show that you are rich in this concern. I'm not laying down the law to you, but because the others have made such an effort, I would also like to see you show how genuine your love is. So on this matter I'm only telling you my own opinion. It's best for you now to complete what you already began last year: not only did you get on with it, but the decision came from you. So now finish off the action, in order that the result also corresponds to what you so readily planned – as far as you had the means. For of course everyone's readiness is most welcome, but depending on what he or she can afford, and no more. I don't intend others to have it easy and you to have difficulties; rather, I want to balance things out: in the present situation your surplus for their deficiency, so that their surplus is also available for your deficiency, to produce equality – as it is written:

'The one with much had no surplus,
and the one with little had no lack.'

But thank God that he filled Titus, too, with such commitment to you that he accepted the commission – indeed, really he's so committed to you that he's making the journey of hs own accord.

With him we're sending brother Tychikos.[166] His good reputation for his work for the gospel is going round all the churches; moreover, he's also been chosen by the churches to accompany us, to check the use of the money which we're to hand over, in order to honour the Lord. That's also just what we want, because at all events we want to avoid the possibility that anyone might suspect us. After all, we're bringing a large sum. So we want to make sure that there aren't any objections, not only before God, but also on the human side.

We're also sending our brother Sosipatros with the two of them.[167] We've often found his industry confirmed in many matters, and now he's all the more ready to commit himself, because he has high hopes of you.

As for Titus, he's my partner and colleague among you. And as for our brothers, they're delegates of the churches, Christ's splendour. So show them your love, and that we've reason to be proud of you. Show them that they represent the churches.[168]

I'm attaching a letter to the brothers and sisters in Achaia, also about the collection.[169] Make sure that it gets passed on to the churches immediately.

Send greetings to Nannos, the shipbuilder, my dear friend. I've come to treasure what he wrote, for you and for himself. I'm looking forward to being able to talk to him and to you soon, not just in letters, but face to face.

The grace of our Lord Jesus be with you all.

Fortunatus, member of the council of elders of the church in Corinth

to

the Church Commission for Collecting and Examining Apostolic Writings, in Rome

Grace and peace to you all!
Reverend brothers, you've enquired whether any other works of the apostle Paul are in our possession which might be suitable

for those seeking baptism and for strengthening the faithful. On behalf of the council of elders of which I am now a member again, I'm enclosing a copy of the rest of the letters of the apostle.

I don't want to anticipate the verdict of the commission as to whether they're appopriate for use in church teaching. But please allow me to report some considerations which influenced us in the council of elders and which may explain to you why we have so far kept these letters from the world-wide church.

As you know, we handed on the first part of Paul's letters to the other churches during his lifetime, because the central teachings of the church can be seen from them: the gospel of the crucifixion and resurrection of the Lord, the tradition of the Lord's supper, the principles of a Christian way of life for men and women, the doctrine of the church as the body of Christ – to mention just the most important passages. In the same way, many copies were immediately made of his letter to the church in Rome, because it contains a summary of his theology. Moreover, Paul wrote it in Corinth in that memorable winter, now more than forty years ago, when he was with us for the last time. This and other letters have long been the common property of all Christians and are read with great profit and used to support the faith, not least in the battle against the variety of heresies which certainly plague you as much as they do us.

However, so far we haven't been able to decide whether to publish the letters that we're now sending to you.[170] They are too much bound up with that decisive crisis which tore apart not only our church but also the apostle himself. Compared with that, our dispute last year in which you kindly intervened from Rome and which you helped us to settle[171] is a harmless family squabble. The young people were discontented with the council of elders and dismissed some of them, including me. I remember that I thought like them when I was still young. It wasn't the death of the church. You gave us tremendous support with your letter at the time and told the young people to behave themselves. So now I'm back in office and respected again. However, at that time, a good forty years ago, more was at stake. The letters which I'm sending will give you an impression of this. They're evidence of a passionate quarrel, and some of the things which Paul wrote probably arose more from his pain and anger than from any intention to add a chapter to a collection of church teaching.

So first of all we kept them as testimony to our personal history. But when you sent your enquiry, we studied the letters thoroughly once again, and noted that for all his militant passion the great apostle wrote amazingly important and central things to us. One might also say that the heat of the conflict in fact inspired Paul to state even more impressively and basically the gospel by which we all live. So we've become convinced that we can no longer keep these writings from the church public. We hope that they may be as much of a blessing to the whole world as they were to us, in that decisive year when Paul came to Corinth for the last time.

Perhaps as one of the few who still have personal experience of it, I may sum up briefly what became of the collection which the apostle mentions often in his letters. Before the onset of winter Paul arrived with the delegates of the churches of Asia and Macedonia to complete the relief work for the Christians in Jerusalem. Titus, along with Tychikos and Sosipatros, had already done the groundwork, so that we and all the churches in the province of Achaia had brought together a considerable treasure.

I shall never forget how important this collection was to the apostle. He spoke in an excited way and with great hopes, though at the same time somewhat anxiously, as if he were afraid that Jerusalem might scorn our gift.[172] He wanted this action to be unmistakable proof that the time announced by the prophets had been fulfilled: all nations were coming to the mountain of God. The Gentiles were bringing their riches. They were no longer excluded from God's salvation, but were bearing the fruits which the spirit had produced among them to the place where the gospel began.

'When this is done,' Paul said, 'I want to complete my commission and take the message of Christ to the western end of the world, to Spain.' At that time he was already preparing for this journey in Corinth; he wrote to the church in Rome to introduce himself and to get the support he needed from it – you'll know his letter.

When winter was over, before Easter, the delegation set off for

Jerusalem: representatives from Asia, Macedonia and Achaia. It was a splendid procession, and they took a substantial gift.

But Paul's hopes weren't fulfilled. While James and the others accepted the gift as welcome help, and felt that they had to recognize that Paul and Titus had kept their promise, they couldn't attach the significance to the enterprise that it was meant to have in the eyes of those who brought the collection. You'll know that Paul was arrested in Jerusalem, waited two years for his trial, and was then sent to Rome. He never reached Spain. In the meantime others have taken up the work there. It must have been a bitter disappointment for him.

His death put us all into deep mourning, and the faith of many of us was severely shaken, because we had counted on Paul being alive to meet his Lord when he came. But when we read his letters, we still hear his voice, the voice of the gospel of Jesus Christ, the crucified one, who lives by God's power.

So we're sending you the rest of the letters. In them God, the Father of our Lord Jesus Christ, is continuing his work, so that people all over the world believe in him and worship him, and if God gives the world yet more years, our children and grandchildren, too.

Greetings from all the elders of Corinth and the whole church Greetings, too, from me, Fortunatus. I confirm with my signature that these writings come from Paul. I pray God that you may make wise decisions.

God bless you.

Appendix

The task

Biblical theology has to do with historical texts which are important for us today although they come from a distant past, and were written in a different language and a different culture. But how can we understand them, as far as possible in their original meaning? If we begin by assuming that Paul has something to say to us, we must first ask what he wanted to say at the time when he was dictating his letters. That raises the question, 'To *whom* did he want to say what he did, and *why?*' In our case, that means that in order to understand Paul we need the Corinthians.

Biblical scholars normally solve the task they face by means of translation, textual analysis and historical research into the setting, and build their explanation on that. In this version of the letters to the Corinthians I am attempting to approach the task by translating and reconstructing letters. In doing so I have used a good deal of imagination: most of the Corinthian women and men whose voices are heard here are purely fictional characters – of necessity, since we know just ten people from the historical community by name, and very little even about them. We know one person's occupation; we know that some of them had 'houses' and were therefore well-to-do; and we hear that a few had been baptized by Paul or had visited him in Ephesus – but most things are left to our imagination.[1] Nevertheless, our imagination is not allowed to run riot, but has to be bound by experience of history. Even exegetes who work along strictly scholarly lines need this kind of controlled imagination: they, too, cannot avoid having some idea of 'the Corinthians' and of the events in the church, because this is the only way in which they can discover what Paul's letters mean. The Pauline texts themselves are the main touchstone here. In them we find, for example, references to the social divisions[2] in the church ('. . . not many wise and learned by the usual standards'), quotations from written remarks ('Now, as to what you've written'), and talk which was going the rounds in Corinth ('because people are saying . . .'). We have answers from which we can infer the questions, attempts at self-defence which indicate what accusations are being made; and not least we can sense annoyance, anger, longing, hurt and other emotions which reflect just how sharp the controversy was. Here New Testament research has been very thorough and has developed well-founded ideas about which groups in Corinth were expressing their views and what events led to the apostle's letters. Here I have tried to build on these results, focus on specific individuals and relate the events in the Corinthian community through their letters.

In the process, many of our present experiences will certainly slip in. We cannot take off our modern spectacles when we come into contact with past ages, and indeed we wouldn't understand anything at all unless we came across something we 'knew'. But my aim is not to translate the events at Corinth into our time, but to indicate what they meant when they happened. If in the process some things emerge which seem to us to be modern and topical, this is partly because the urban society of the first centuries displays some similarities with our present-day society. A port worker of our time would probably come to an agreement with his counterparts Lykos and Nannos about the most important questions of life, and businesswomen like Chloe or Phoibe could join in the small talk of modern merchants without difficulty – provided that they understood the language and could bridge the gap in time.

So I have attempted to look for the people of Corinth where they lived, to get to know them as well as possible and formulate their letters. In this appendix I want to indicate how I have combined scholarship and imagination, and where the dividing lines are.

The chronology

The dates suggested in the letters of Paul and Acts, combined with historical information from other sources, allow us to define quite precisely when Paul was in Corinth and when he wrote his letters. An imperial inscription found in Delphi contains information about the period during which Gallio, who is mentioned in Acts 18.12–17, held office. Gallio, the philosopher Seneca's brother, was proconsul of the province of Achaia in 51/52. Paul was brought before him by representatives of the synagogue. A few days later Paul ended his first stay in Corinth (Acts 18.18). This fixed historical point enables us to define the chronological sequence of events as follows:

Paul came to Corinth for the first time in autumn 49 or 50. He remained there for eighteen months (Acts 18.11), i.e. until spring 51 or 52. After that he worked for about three years either in Ephesus or in Asia Minor, with Ephesus as a base. Paul was in Corinth for the last time in winter 55/56, and then in spring 56 travelled with the collection to Jerusalem. The conflict reflected in II Corinthians must have occurred immediately before that, i.e. presumably in summer or autumn 55. Paul could have written the letters contained in I Corinthians in spring 54 or 55, some time before Pentecost (I Cor.16.8).[3] In working on the correspondence I have opted for the second possibility, so that the whole history of the letter takes place in a year, from spring to winter 55, and the correspondence from I Corinthians moves directly into the controversies of II Corinthians.[4] The connection between the two collections of letters supports this. Even if we assume that the opponents in II Corinthians are not the same as those in I Corinthians,[5] the beginnings of the conflict which develops in II Corinthians can already be seen in I Corinthians, and this suggests a very close connection between the content of the two parts. But it would also be possible to date I Corinthians earlier and thus have a longer interval between the two sets of correspondence.

Precisely what happened in 55 between Paul and the church in Corinth is connected with the question just how many individual letters the two letters to the Corinthians which have come down to us contain, and in what order they were written.

The hypothesis that the letters to the Corinthians are made up of different bits of text was put forward more than 200 years ago by Johann Salomo Semler (1725–1791), and since then it has been constantly discussed.[6] In the meantime widespread agreement has been reached among New Testament scholars that there are other composite collections among the letters of the New Testament, in other words that the early church put together numbers of letters of Paul to form longer 'letters'. This is also conjectured e.g. for Philippians, and the question also arises over the two letters to the Corinthians.

When it comes to identifying individual letters, there is a quite simple and conclusive solution for II Corinthians. Günther Bornkamm put this forward[7] and at the same time described the dramatic course of the controversy. In his view, II Corinthians contains five letters: the 'apologia', 2.14–7.4; the 'tearful letter', 10–13; the 'letter of reconciliation', 1.1–2.13 + 7.5–16; and two 'collection letters', 8 and 9. The order in which they were written follows from a reconstruction of the course of the events which are echoed in the text. On hearing the news of the arrival and activity of new apostles, Paul first of all wrote a moderate letter in his defence, the 'apologia'; after that he travelled to Corinth in person and met with failure there. The 'tearful letter' is a reaction to this defeat, which wounded him deeply. This letter and Titus' visit to Corinth made the community think again, so Paul could write the 'letter of reconciliation' in deep gratitude. At that time he was already on his way through Macedonia in support of the collection. The two 'collection letters' belong in this context. The text provides a series of convincing pointers and references to confirm this this hypothetical division, e.g. II Cor.2.10–13. Cf. also the numerous allusions to the appearance of other apostles in the 'tearful letter', II Cor.10–13.

On the basis of this reconstruction, a purely technical explanation of the present form of the text of II Corinthians could be that the original letters of Paul were arranged in the wrong order, and that one of them came to be put between the pages of another letter: the 'apologia' between 2.13 and 7.5 of the 'letter of reconciliation'. The abrupt ending of the description of Paul's journey in 2.13 and its equally abrupt continuation at 7.5 indicates an interruption at this point. However, Bornkamm does not presuppose that the letters were mixed up by mistake, but assumes that the person who put together the letters to form a single letter had a deliberate plan. This is also suggested by the fact that the beginnings and ends of the letters have been omitted, with the exception of those which introduce and conclude II Corinthians in its present form.

How many part-letters there are in I Corinthians is less clear. On the one hand there are good reasons for also assuming a collection of letters here. Johannes Weiss already remarked that 'we no longer have copies of the originals of Paul's letters, but only copies of a collection made by the church'.[8] He comes to the conclusion that I Corinthians could be made up of two or three letters. For example, the first four chapters seem like a coherent letter, which also begins a concluding passage after 4.14. There are also breaks in the the text; for example, ch.9 begins a new topic directly after the remarks about sacrifices to idols in ch.8 and then returns to the first topic – at the latest by 10.14. Besides, in I Corinthians Paul discusses a wealth of different topics, each of which in itself could have occupied a whole letter, but which equally well could have been parts of one long letter. I Corinthians 5.9 poses a special problem: here Paul refers to a letter which he wrote earlier. Has this 'earlier letter' disappeared? Or is it part of I Corinthians?

These questions led Weiss and other scholars after him to reconstruct the original part-letters. However, the results prove very complicated: I Corinthians is cut into many pieces to make up three or four letters. Each time this presupposes that the early Christian redaction of I Corinthians did the same jig-saw puzzle in the opposite direction.[9]

On the other hand, some New Testament scholars regard the whole of I Corinthians as a unity.[10] There are also good reasons for this.[11] The different sections do not indicate a dramatic progress in the action, as they do in II Corinthians.[12] They could also have stood side by side in a single letter as answers to a series of enquiries.

I have decided also to divide I Corinthians into four letters, and in addition to interrupt two part-letters by 'pauses in dictation'.

The main reason for this is to make the correspondence more readable: the wealth of content can be coped with better by a more frequent to-ing and fro-ing of letters than by a whole mass of inquiries and an equally full response from Paul.

However, I have left the order of the part-letters as they have come down to us in I Corinthians. I was able to take full account of the breaks and linked units which conjectural reconstructions have worked out even with the order unchanged. I have assumed that 1.1–5.8, the text which immediately precedes 5.9, is the 'earlier letter', which with its 'appendix' in 5.1–8 provides sufficient reason for the misunderstanding that Paul puts right in 5.9ff.[13]

Wherever the division has produced letters without a greeting and a conclusion, I have added these. On the basis of other letters of Paul and their structure[14] I have attempted to make the beginnings and ends of the letters as 'Pauline' as posisble, since if there are any part-letters in I and II Corinthians, then of course originally they all had a greeting and an ending. Each time I have indicated the seams by a note.

At three points I have omitted verses. Exegetes are largely unanimous that two of these passages are later insertions: I Cor.14.33b–36 ('As in all the churches of the saints, women are to keep silent in church . . .') and II Cor.6.14–7.1 ('Do not submit to a strange yoke with unbelievers . . .'). These two texts clearly interrupt the context and on closer analysis of the content and style prove to be insertions by another hand.[15]

In content, the third passage, I Cor.15.56, could come from Paul, but it really looks like a later explanation of the song of victory which Paul strikes up in I Cor.15.54b–55, 'The sting of death is sin, the power of sin is the law.'[16] It seems to me more logical that in the original version of his letter Paul added the song of victory over death immediately, without an intervening explanation of the thanksgiving for victory (v.47).

Finally, I have not included one whole chapter in the correspondence: II Cor.9. This is a letter about the collection, with the same concerns as II Cor.8, but addressed to the churches of Achaia.[17]

At three points in the texts which have come down to us (II Cor.8.18; 8.22; 12.18), evidently the names of 'brothers' were originally given but have been deleted for reasons unknown to us. To get nearer to the original form of the letter I have inserted names.

Apart from the passages mentioned, I have taken over unabbreviated the whole of the text of the letters to the Corinthians as it has come down to us in the New Testament.

The translation

Principles

By his own account, Paul writes 'nothing but what you can read and understand' (II Cor.1.13). In other words, he expects his letters to be plainly understandable to the recipients and not to need any additional explanation. So the translation must aim to get as close as possible to this immediate understandability. I have therefore attempted to translate the texts into the kind of language that I would use today in a letter to good friends about something that was personally important to me. Often this is possible by direct translation, but where a word-for-word rendering of the original sense tends to distort it for us, I have looked for freer expressions to render the content more precisely. Occasionally I have found brief expansions necessary to convey the sense. Major additions and alterations are always indicated in the notes; smaller expansions like 'in any case', 'really', 'no' and so on are not specially indicated.

Of course every translation is at the same time an interpretation. It is no longer possible for us to decide what some passages mean; experts argue over this. In such instances it is no advantage to render the texts in an ambiguous or vague way, to keep them open for every possible interpretation. We can assume that Paul wanted to express himself clearly. So the translation must opt for one meaning and express this as clearly as possible. I have referred in the notes to the most important of the controversial translation problems.

The style of Paul's letters is complex. He uses both everyday language and solemn liturgical forms of speech; he writes highly poetic verses and the next moment adopts a telegraphic style; he formulates polished sentences, and at other places mixes up sentence-construction and grammar. All this should appear in the translation as far as possible, since 'style does not stand alongside "content" . . . but forms a unity with the "content"'.[18] So as a rule I have not completed unfinished sentences and have expanded brief expressions which are concentrated on essential key words only where this has seemed to me to be absolutely necessary for understanding. For any particular style is a 'clear reflection of the internal situation of the apostle with its moods and feelings'.[19] Of course there are limits to such stylistic translation. The subtler features like word-plays, colouring or rhythms can only be approximated in another language.[20]

Word families which are difficult to translate: 'flesh', 'boast', 'service'

Two terms which occupy a key position in the letters to the Corinthians cause great difficulties for translators: *sarx* ('flesh') and *kauchasthai* ('boast'). There is no comparable expression for either root in our language which can cover the breadth of meanings and their particular focuses.

Sarx, sarkikos, sarkinos is traditionally translated 'flesh' or 'fleshly'. The words mean different things, depending on the context.

1. In the Old Testament, and largely also in the New Testament, this group primarily serves to denote the human, the body, natural earthly existence, as e.g. in II Cor.4.11: 'in our mortal flesh' = 'in our mortal existence' (parallel 4.10, 'in our body').

2. But Paul can also use 'flesh' to denote our sinful existence, in contrast to the 'spiritual' life which is justified by God, thus especially in Galatians and in Romans (Gal.5–6; Rom.7–8). As far as I can see, this terminology does not appear explicitly in the letters to the Corinthians.

3. In Corinth, the terms were used in yet a different way, namely to denote different stages of experience of God. In I Cor.3.1 Paul begins by explaining to the Corinthians, who evidently see themselves as being on a higher level, that he has been able to talk with them only 'as with fleshly and not as with

spiritual', and he interprets these terms by using the image of chldren who can only take milk and not yet any adult food. His opponents use the terms to disparage Paul and his colleagues: they themselves presented the 'spiritual', overpoweringly religious, character of the gospel, dismissing Paul as an inferior preacher whose speech and experience are not filled with the spirit and who therefore can speak and act only 'according to the flesh'. By contrast, in II Cor.10.2 Paul defends himself and turns the tables on them, accusing them of boasting 'after the flesh' (II Cor.11.18). (Here we have echoes of the use of 'fleshly' = 'godless', familiar from the letters to the Romans and the Galatians.)

I have not found a really appropriate word to express what is meant by 'flesh' here. I have made do with 'ordinary', 'quite human', 'worldly', and 'after the manner of the world'.

While the translation 'boast', verb and noun, is not wrong for *kauchasthai*, *kauchesis* and *kauchema*, it cannot cover the breadth of meaning of these words. This 'multi-level term . . . describes the problem of self-awareness and dealing with it'.[21] The translation has to make do with a number of expressions like 'allege', 'impose', 'extol', 'enthuse', 'put in the right light', 'claim validity' and 'pride', 'bragging', 'showing off', 'reputation' and so on. I have used the term 'boast' which runs through most translations of the Bible only at two points, where Paul himself is quoting from the Old Testament. It is a pity to have lost the use of a single expression, but in the interests of comprehensibility that is unavoidable.

There are also problems with the words *diakonia*, *diakonia*, *diakonein* and *diakonos*, usually translated as 'service', 'serve' and 'servant'. This rendering is misleading in that it suggests humble submission and modesty, whereas *diakonos* is more a title of honour. Anyone who is given a *diakonia* is the fully authorized representative of the one who has bestowed this charge. Paul's opponents boast of being '*diakonoi*',[22] and Paul goes on to emphasize the splendour and glory of his *diakonia*. The best rendering in English seems to be 'commission', but unfortunately there is no appropriate parallel noun, so here again paraphrase has been necessary.[23]

Anyone who wants to follow the way in which the words mentioned above appear in the original text can do this with the help of earlier translations like the King James (Authorized) Version or the Revised Version. In them one and the same word always stands for the Greek terms, i.e. 'flesh' and 'fleshly', 'boast' and 'boasting', 'servant' and 'service'.

Fixed terms: gospel, apostle, church

I have taken over words which had already become fixed terms in the earliest Christian terminology as loan words, or rendered them in the current English translation.

Gospel (*euangelion*) means in the original Greek 'good news', 'joyful message'; in the New Testament it denotes the message of Christ, i.e. the content and act of preaching.

The term 'apostle' was already being used as an evocative title in the time of Paul, but not with the fixed meaning that it acquired later, e.g. in Acts. *Apostolos* means 'emissary', 'ambassador', 'messenger'. At the time of the letters to the Corinthians the title alone did not yet say who had done the sending. Paul emphasizes that he was 'not sent from men, nor through a man, but through Jesus Christ' (Gal.1.1). He bases his office as apostle on his calling by the risen Christ, and in so doing sets himself alongside the other apostles who were witnesses of the resurrection (I Cor.9.1; 15.3–10). But he also calls the brothers chosen by the churches to bring the collection 'apostles' of the churches (II Cor.8.23).[24] Here I have translated the term 'delegates', whereas in the case of Paul, his opponents and other itinerant preachers I have adopted 'apostle' as a title.

The Greek word *ekklesia* is originally a political term and means 'popular assembly'. But it has become a fixed term for Christian communities, both for the smaller groups which met in the houses (Aquila and Prisca send greetings from Ephesus 'together with the *ekklesia* in their house', I Cor.16.19) and for the whole *ekklesia* in a city. Here 'church' is clearly the most versatile rendering.

Titles, names, forms of address: Christ, Lord, brothers and sisters

The form in which Christians living today speak about or to Christ seems to me to be very important. In the form of address, in the use and the sound of his name, we express the nature of our relationship to him, confess what we expect and hope of him, what he means to us. So when translating I must ask how the traditional titles and names of Jesus Christ can come to mean for present-day readers what they meant at that time for Paul and the Christians in Corinth.

Here there seem to me to be problems over translating the title 'kyrios'. 'Lord' is an inadequate rendering. With this title the first Christians were honouring Christ as the only norm 'in a world in which very different lords were claiming lordship over men and women'.[25] When they rejoiced in their Lord, their joy also implied the opposite to current gestures of lordship. For them, the Kyrios was not only *over* all lords; he was also *other* than all lords. Paul indicates a tender relationship when, for example, he longs 'to be away from the body and at home with *the Lord*' (II Cor.5.8). In contrast to that, many of us associate the title 'lord' with male domination, the exercise of power, and subjection, and this leads women in particular to avoid the form of address 'Lord' completely. But I have not found a more appropriate word, and the loan word 'Kyrios' would not resolve the difficulty either. So I hope that the original significance of this title will also be detectable from the way in which Paul and the Corinthians call on their Lord.

Paul often uses the name 'Christ' as a proper name, and sometimes also as a title, as the Greek translation of 'Messiah'. In such cases I use the article: 'as the body . . . so also the Christ' (I Cor.12.12). This also corresponds to Paul's usage: he too marks 'the Christ' as a title by the article, and moreover puts the article before the name in certain phrases using the genitive.[26]

I also want to point out the limits of the possibility of translating the Pauline 'in Christ' (*en Christo*) and 'in the Lord' (*en kyrio*). Paul uses these terms very often and in different contexts to depict the relationship of the individual or the community to Christ, the 'new principle of life'[27] in communion with him. If one wanted to express the meaning more precisely, one would have to resort to periphrases, from the general 'in the church sphere', 'in a Christian sense' to the literal notion of incorporation 'in the body of Christ'. I have taken over the formulae 'in Christ' and 'in the Lord'. This recurrent form reflects a peculiarity of Paul's language.

The way in which the members of the community are addressed is also of far-reaching significance. Paul addresses them as *adelphoi*, and in all the translations of the Bible I know this is rendered 'brothers'. This one-sidedly male form of address has been adopted and continued in countless church texts and addresses, and sometimes one can still hear it today.

In Greek 'brother' is *adelphos* and 'sister' *adelphe*. The masculine plural is used for both 'brothers' and 'brothers and sisters'.[28] This terminology certainly does not meet our present-day concern for inclusive language. The translation 'brothers' does not do justice to the fact that Paul addresses his letters to men and women equally. This is indicated by the lists of greetings (e.g. Rom.16) and I Cor.7, in which Paul speaks of men and women in the singular and each time mentions 'the brothers' and 'the sisters' side by side. I have therefore always translated *adelphoi* as 'brothers and sisters' when it is used as a form of address to the community.

Practical suggestions

For teachers and others who work either professionally or – like Paul – as unpaid volunteers with biblical texts and want to use this book in services, Bible weeks, discussion groups or in teaching, here are some practical suggestions.

Aim

My work on the letters to the Corinthians arose out of the experience that the Pauline texts begin to take on new life when I read them in the context of their history. The first time I had this experience was when I read II Corinthians straight through at a sitting in the order reconstructed by Günther Bornkamm. I would like everyone to have had this experience, particularly those whose work involves the Bible. So the following practical suggestions focus on the experience of the wider context of the whole story in order to restore their original dynamic to individual texts, to experience Paul acting and reacting, and through this to understand what he is fighting for, what he is arguing against, what are his concerns, what drives him to present the gospel as he does.

Understanding the text as part of history

This is really not a method but an extension of my own concern with the wider context. If we ourselves have experienced the whole story and made it part of ourselves, this will automatically be communicated to those with whom we work. Of course we will continue to preach 'pericopes', discuss sections, meditate on individual verses. But now we will read aloud, narrate and interpret the part against the background of the whole. We shall be able to sketch the setting in a few sentences, and that will enable people to enter into things with their own histories. Some interpreters seem to be afraid that they will simply prevent hearers from getting personally involved if they keep to what happened at the time. My experience is different: the more clearly I see and identify the original situation in a section of the Bible, the more naturally the text also links up with experiences of life today.

Reading whole letters aloud

Longer passages of text are all too seldom read or read aloud in church work. There is a fear of making too many demands on the hearers. But by thinking that the congregation or group can take only short extracts and that these must have detailed explanations, we are merely endorsing the prejudice that the Bible is a collection of almost incomprehensible texts. I think that the essentials of any of the ten part-letters of Paul to the Corinthians, read as a unit, can be understood immediately. Of course some details will escape the audience, but the content will come through sufficiently for them to be able to follow the broad outline, and this brings more gain for the understanding than loss from the details that are missed.

I can imagine a sermon on I Cor.12–14, for example, going like this:

1. Five minutes preliminary explanation. What was the situation in Corinth? There was a hierarchy of religious experience; speaking in tongues came top of the list, and those who could do it seemed to be nearest to God. Speaking with tongues is probably alien to us, but what about the hierarchy? Which people in church are regarded as 'outstanding Christians' and which are 'on the edge'? The explanations aim to link the group with the Christians in Corinth. What were their problems, conflicts and questions, and what are ours?

2. Anyone who can read well reads out I Cor.12–14 straight through.

3. Pause for reflection.

4. Invitation to a discussion after the sermon: according to Paul's letter about the many different kinds of spiritual gift, one can expect that many people will make some contribution.

It is important for the reader to prepare well. He or she must be so steeped in the text that the written sentences really do become the spoken word. This is best achieved if one makes oneself so familiar with the content both emotionally and in terms of the subject-matter that one not only knows but also feels what one is saying. Anyone who reads the tearful letter (II Cor.10–13) aloud may well fight off tears. At any rate, readers must be so thoroughly involved in the text that they feel the insult against Paul, his desperate rage, his disappointment and his anxiety in his sentences. If that happens, these four lengthy chapters will not become too long and too much for anyone, and even those who have never heard or read a word of Paul will grasp the essential point.

This is not a tactic for generating tension and thus 'selling' a biblical text better ('Not like so many who peddle God's word', II Cor.2.17). No, Paul's tension, his feelings, suffering and passion are part of his theology. They belong indissolubly to his preaching, and are anything but an addition to his method ('We refuse to play any tricks or to tamper with God's word', II Cor.4.2). Paul is sharing himself when he is preaching the gospel. He never detaches the message from his own existence. Therefore it is our task not only to reflect on his letters but also to live them and let them become our experience.

Letting the brothers and sisters in Corinth have their say

We also need to pay attention to the original recipients of the letters of Paul, since they are the ones to whom Paul is referring. He is addressing them, and so they can help us to understand his letters. Consequently I have allowed them a say in the correspondence, and of course their letters, too, can be used to put the related letter from Paul in the context of the discussion. Why shouldn't Krispos, the former president of the synagogue, appear at a service, introduce himself briefly to the congregation, and read out the first part of his letter (62ff.) – as an introduction to I Cor.12–14?

Some letters have been written by a number of Corinthian men and women and reflect the discussion among the writers. This can be turned into a scene: there are all kinds of possibilities, from dividing the reading between different speakers to acting out the dispute. The church's second letter to Paul (114ff.), for example, is almost a model for this: one need only use the interpolations by Tertius as stage instructions and assign the parts.

Getting role-play going

Groups which are good at acting will want to go a stage further: they will assign roles, and then each character will study the content of his or her own text in order to be able to enter into the action freely. The basic text will not be repeated literally, but will serve as identification for the role, as a means of getting to know the characteristics and views of the character in question. After this preparation the actors can begin to interact. The scene develops out of the interplay.

A group which has struggled over the letter to Paul by acting it out will eagerly await his answer, since all are now involved; they have so to speak themselves become the church of Corinth, and what indiduals have played out and seen will have points of contact with experiences from their own life today, since every actor also brings himself or herself into the play. The play becomes fragments of experience shared between us and Paul.

Such experiences can then be exchanged and discussed: what happened to me 'in Corinth' and what does Paul's letter sound like now? It is already possible to integrate Paul into the play, for example by using a three-act structure:

Act 1: Dispute or discussion of the Corinthians on writing the letter.

Act 2: Paul's answer arrives and is read out.

Act 3: Reactions to Paul's letter: joy, disappointment, criticism, confirmation, new dispute, further letter, etc.

Becoming conversation partners

Regardless of whether the events at Corinth are read out, played out or improvised, their function is and remains to reconstruct the conflict against the background of which Paul needs to be seen if he is to be understood. His original conversation partners are the Christians of the time, but we men and women of today are also his conversation partners, as with our faith, our need for clarification or even our scepticism we expect something from Paul – or are simply sitting curiously on the 'visitors' bench'. And just as the church in Corinth was a varied and colourful community, so we and our contemporaries differ, and the conversation with Paul can develop in a similarly varied way. The Corinthian church offers us its own multiplicity, so that we can see our different approaches to Paul.

In terms of method, that means that we should make sure that everyone finds a place in the colourful society of the Corinthians. Where, with whom, in what corner, shall I take part in the event? One person may feel like Chrysallis, one share the view of Quartus, another perhaps find Xenia quite intolerable, another feel rebuffed by Melas, another suffer with Mara. In one way or another, everyone will feel something at various points.

The tensions between the people in Corinth will be reflected in the group. So individuals will discuss different things with Paul. And again, Paul can take that: he was a controversial apostle, and remains one after almost two thousand years, one who provokes very different reactions. So he is still alive, even today. He becomes lifeless, abstract and threatening if we put him on a pedestal and make him a 'super-apostle' who we know was always right.

So in order to find conversation partners for Paul we should stimulate the members of our group or church to find their personal place among the brothers and sisters of Corinth. The following questions could help here.

On the events: What is alien to me? What seems familiar? What moves me, recalls my own experiences?

On the characters: To which of the Corinthian women and men do I feel close, perhaps akin? Who continues to be incomprehensible to me, stimulates me, offends me?

And finally, when everyone has found a place, to Paul. How do I hear him speaking, from my standpoint? And how do the others hear him? What does he say to them? And what does he say to me? What do they say to him? And what do I say to him?

In this way the controversy with Paul takes on the polyphony which it orignally had: every woman and man encounters this apostle and his interpretation of the message of Christ with her or his own history.

Writing letters

Finally I would like to add something more about the methods of Bible study that I have used in this book. Anyone can join in the correspondence with Paul by writing a letter, and stimulate others to do so. The approach here need not always be historical. Just as Paul speaks to us through his letters over two thousand years, so we can write back to him over time from our day and in our own words; we can read one of his letters as though it were addressed directly to us and as individuals, or even in small teams, we can write him a reply. After that we can read our letters aloud to one another: this will result in a whole range of individual answers, reactions, criticisms, enquiries. Here questions are once again put to Paul; his texts will now begin to speak more personally to us. Some will offend us; in some cases he will still owe us an answer; in some cases he will comfort us, stimulate us and help us.

A group which does not already know Paul almost by heart can attempt to write a letter from the apostle and reply to the enquiries from the church in Corinth. For information the members of the group can be given a letter from the Corinthians, e.g. the report of the first appearance of the new apostles (84ff.). Now they move to Ephesus and become Paul and his fellow workers: they have received the letter and want to compose an answer. What will the content be? Perhaps just the material will be collected, some ideas which Paul could have written or which 'we' would write to this community, perhaps also a letter or several letters. At all events, afterwards the group will eagerly compare its own results with the letter which the real Paul wrote in this situation. Here the attraction lies in the discovery of the difference. We replied like this – and Paul replied like that. Why? What moved him to react in such a different way from us?

If this exercise is suitable for those who do not know much about Paul, what follows is more for experts. A letter from Paul can be rewritten in such a way as to take up our present-day questions and problems. This is a demanding task. In the last resort that is true of any interpretation of the Bible. The demanding part is not so much the method: it is not particularly difficult to formulate a concern as a letter of Paul. What is demanding is the content, if Paul is really to have his say: what would the Paul whom we know from his letters say to the unresolved problems which concern us today in church and society? To get closer to our aim it is not enough to present our own ideas in an apostolic tone and decorate them with a few quotations. As often happens, sayings of Paul can be used as proof texts for a quite 'un-Pauline' view. Already shortly after his death, still in the New Testament period, Paul had been depicted in a form in which he probably would not have recognized himself, and letters were written in his name by his disciples which he would hardly have written himself. They may have been important and useful for later Christians, but all attempts to compose a letter in the name of Paul must be measured by the original, by the passionate remarks of Paul himself. I'm not writing this as a deterrent. What is left for us representatives of the gospel, if not to attempt time and again to let Paul (or Mark, John, Hosea or Jeremiah) speak in such a way that they proclaim their message in our situation? We shall be only partially successful in meeting this demand. Nevertheless, it remains our task constantly to address anew the gospel which Paul fulfilled, inspired, promoted, in our own language to our fellow men and women in their situation.

Bibliography

1. Technical theological and historical studies

S.Arai, 'Die Gegner des Paulus im I.Korintherbrief und das Problem des Gnosis', *NTS* 19, 1972/73, 430–7

K.Berger, 'Apostelbrief und apostolische Rede', *ZNW* 1974, 190–231

H.D.Betz, *Second Corinthians 8 and 9*, Hermeneia, Philadelphia 1986

G.Bornkamm, 'The More Excellent Way (1.Kor.13)', in *Early Christian Experience*. London and New York 1969, 180–94

– , 'On the Understanding of Worship', ibid., 161–79

– , 'Lord's Supper and Church in Paul', ibid., 123–60

– , 'Das missionarische Verhalten des Paulus nach 1.Kor 9.19–23 und in der Apostelgeschichte', in *Geschichte und Glaube* II, *Gesammelte Aufsätze* IV, 1971, 149–61

– , 'Die Vorgeschichte des sogenannten Zweiten Korintherbriefes', ibid., 162–94

U.Borse, ' "Tränenbrief" und 1.Korintherbrief', *SNTU* 9, 1984, 175–202

H.Conzelmann, 'Korinth und die Mädchen der Aphrodite', in *Theologie als Schriftauslegung*, 1974, 152–66

G.Dautzenberg, 'Zum religionsgeschichtlichen Hintergrund von *diakrisis pneumaton* (1.Kor 12.10)', *BZ* 15, 1971, 93–104

– , *Urchristliche Prophetie. Ihre Erforschung, ihre Voraussetzungen und ihre Struktur im 1.Kor*, BWANT 104, 1975

G.Delling, 'Nun aber sind sie heilig (1.Kor 7.14)', in *Studien zum Neuen Testament und zum hellenistischen Judentum*, 1970, 257–87

S.Dickey, 'Some Economic and Social Conditions of Asia Minor

Affecting the Expansion of Christianity', in *Studies in Early Christianity presented to F.C.Porter and B.W.Bacon*, ed. S. J. Case, New York and London 1928, 393–416

C.Dietzfelbinger, *Die Berufung des Paulus als Ursprung seiner Theologie*, WMANT 58, 1985

– , *Das apostolische Selbstbewusstsein des Paulus*, seminar on II Cor. 2.14–7.4, summer semester 1986, unpublished manuscript

– , *Der Kampf des Paulus gegen die Irrlehrer in Korinth*, seminar on II Cor.10–13, winter semester 1986/87, unpublished manuscript

H.-J.Eckstein, *Der Begriff Syneidesis bei Paulus*, WUNT 2.R, 10, 1983

U.Fischer, *Eschatologie und Jenseitserwartung im hellenistichen Diasporajudentum*, BZNW 44, 1978

G.Friedrich, 'Amt und Lebensführung. Eine Auslegung von 2.Kor 6.1–10', *BSt* 39, 1963

– , 'Die Gegner des Paulus im 2.Korintherbrief', in *Auf das Wort kommt es an*, Gesammelte Aufsätze, 1978, 189–223

– , 'Christus, Einheit und Norm der Christen. Das Grundmotiv des 1.Korintherbriefs', ibid., 147.

– , 'Die Kirche Gottes in Korinth', ibid., 132

D.Georgi, *Die Geschichte der Kollekte des Paulus für Jerusalem*, ThF 38, 1963

– , *Die Gegner des Paulus im 2.Korintherbrief*, WMANT 11, 1964

F.Hahn, 'Die alttestamentlichen Motive in der urchristlichen Abendmahlsüberlieferung', *EvTh* 27, 1967, 337–74

– , 'Das Ja des Paulus und das Ja Gottes', in *Neues Testament und christlicher Existenz, FS H.Braun*, 1973, 229–39

– , 'Der Apostolat im Urchristentum', *KuD* 10, 1974, 54–78

M.Hengel, 'Der Kreuzestod Jesu Christi als Gottes souveräne Erlösungstat. Exegese über 2.Korinther 5,11–21', *Theologie und Kirche* 1967, 60–86

– , *Crucifixion*, London and Philadelphia 1977

O.Hofius, 'Erwägungen zur Gestalt und Herkunft des paulinischen Versöhnungsgedankens', *ZThK* 77, 1980, 186–99

J.C.Hurd, *The Origin of I Corinthians*, London 1965

N.Hyldahl, 'Die Frage nach der literarischen Einheit des Zweiten

Korintherbriefes', ZNW 64, 1973, 289–306

J.Jervell, 'Der schwache Charismatiker', in *Rechtfertigung. FS E.Käsemann*, 1976, 185–98

– , 'Die Zeichen des Apostels. Die Wunder beim lukanischen und paulinischen Paulus', *SNTU* 4, 1979, 54–75

E.A.Judge, 'The Early Christians as a Scholastic Community', *Journal of Religious History* 1, 1960–61, 4–15, 125–37

E.Käsemann, 'Die Legitimität des Apostels', ZNW 41, 1942, 33–71

– , 'The Pauline Doctrine of the Lord's Supper', in *Essays on New Testament Themes*, London 1964, 108–35

– , 'Ministry and Community in the New Testament', ibid., 63–94

– , '1.Korinther 2,6–16', in *Exegetische Versuche und Besinnungen* I, 1960, 267–76

– , '1. Korinther 6, 19–20', ibid., 276–9

– , 'Sentences of Holy Law in the New Testament', in *New Testament Questions of Today*, London and Philadelphia 1969, 66–81

– , 'A Pauline Version of the "Amor Fati"', ibid., 217–35

C.D.Lee, 'Social Unrest and Primitive Christianity', in *The Catacombs and the Collosseum*, ed. Stephen Benko and John J.O'Rourke, Valley Forge, Pa. 1971 and London 1972

D.Lührmann, 'Wo man nicht mehr Sklave oder Freier ist. Überlegung zur Struktur frühchristlicher Gemeinden', *WuD*, NF 13, 1975, 53–83

K.Maly, *Mündige Gemeinde. Untersuchungen zur pastoralen Führung des Apostels Paulus im 1.Korintherbrief*, SBM 2, 1962

C.Maurer, 'Ehe und Unzucht nach 1.Kor 6,12–7,7', *WuD*, NF 6, 1959, 159–69

O.F.A.Meinardus, *Paulus in Griechenland*, Athens [3]1990

K.Niederwimmer, 'Erkennen und Lieben. Gedanken zum Verhältnis von Gnosis und Agape im ersten Korintherbrief', *KuD* 11, 1965, 75–102

– , 'Zur Analyse der asketischen Motivation in 1.Kor 7', *ThLZ* 99, 1974, 242–7

– , *Askese und Mysterium. Über Ehe, Ehescheidung und Eheverzicht in den Anfängen des christlichen Glaubens*, FRLANT 13, 1975

W.H.Ollrog, *Paulus und seine Mitarbeiter*, Neukirchen 1979

N.Paphatzis, *Das antike Korinth. Die Museen von Korinth, Isthmia und Sikyon*, Athens 1985

W.Rebell, *Neutestamentliche Apokryphen und Apostolische Väter*, 1992

W.Schenk, 'Der 1.Korintherbrief als Briefsammlung', ZNW 60, 1969, 219–41

W.Schmithals, *Die Gnosis in Korinth. Eine Untersuchung zu den Korintherbriefen*, FRLANT 66, ³1969

– , 'Die Korintherbriefe als Briefsammlung', ZNW 64, 1973, 263–88

W.Schrage, 'Die Stellung zur Welt bei Paulus, Epiktet und in der Apokalyptik', ZThK 61, 1964, 125–54

A.Schreiber, *Die Gemeinde in Korinth. Versuch einer gruppendynamischen Betrachtung der Entwicklung der Gemeinde von Korinth auf der Basis des ersten Korintherbriefes*, NTA, NF 12, 1977

E.Schüssler Fiorenza, *In Memory of Her. A Feminist Reconstruction of Christian Origins*, London and New York 1983

J.H.Schütz, 'Charisma and Social Reality in Primitive Christianity', *Journal of Religion* 54, 1974, 51–70

R.Scranton, I.W.Shaw and L.Ibrahim, *Kenchreai. Eastern Part of Corinth*, I, *Topography and Architecture*, 1978

G.Sellin, 'Das Geheimnis der Weisheit und das Rätsel der Christuspartei', ZNW 73, 1982, 69–96

– , 'I Korinther 5–6 und der "Vorbrief" nach Korinth: Indizien für eine Mehrschichtigkeit von Kommunkationsakten im 1.Korintherbrief', NTS 1991, 535–58

P.Stuhlmacher, 'Das Auferstehungszeugnis nach 1.Kor 15,1–20', *Theologie und Kirche*, 1967, 33–59

G.Theissen, 'Soziale Schichtung in der korinthischen Gemeinde', ZNW 65, 1974, 232–721

– , 'Soziale Integration und sakramentales Handeln', NT 24, 1962, 179–206

– , 'Soteriologische Symbolik in den paulinischen Schriften', KuD 20, 1974, 282–304

– , 'Die Starken und Schwachen in Korinth', EvTh 35, 1975, 155–72

– , 'Legitimität und Lebensunterhalt', NTS 21, 1975, 192–221

– , *Psychological Aspects of Pauline Theology*, Edinburgh and

Philadelphia 1987

– , *The First Followers of Jesus*, London 1978 (US title, *The Sociology of Earliest Palestinian Christianity*, Philadelphia 1978)

K.Thraede, 'Ärger mit der Freiheit. Die Bedeutung von Frauen in Theorie und Praxis der alten Kirche', in G.Scharffenroth and K.Thraede, *'Freunde in Christus werden'. Die Beziehung von Mann und Frau als Frage an Theologie und Kirche, Kennzeichen*, Vol.1, 1977, 31–182

H.Thyen, '"...nicht mehr männlich und weiblich..." Eine Studie zu Galater 3,28', in F.Crüsemann and H.Thyen, *Als Mann und Frau geschaffen. Exegetische Studien zur Rolle der Frau*, 1978, 190–201

P.Veyne, 'Das Römische Reich', in P.Aries and G.Duby (eds.), *Geschichte des privaten Lebens*, Vol.1, *Vom römischen Imperium zum Byzantinischen Reich*, Frankfurt am Main 1989

P.Vielhauer, 'Paulus und die Kephaspartei in Korinth', *NTS* 21, 1974/75, 341–52

U.Wilckens, *Weisheit und Torheit. Eine exegetisch-religionsgeschichtliche Studie zu 1.Kor 1 und 2*, BTh 26, 1959

R.L.Wilken, 'Collegia, Philosophical Schools, and Theology', in *The Catacombs and the Collosseum*, Valley Forge, Pa. 1971 and London 1972

J.Zmijewski, *Der Stil der paulinischen 'Narrenrede'*, BBB 52, 197

2. Commentaries and reference works

W.F.Arndt and F.W.Gingrich, *Greek-English Dictionary of the New Testament*, Chicago 1957

R.Bultmann, *Der zweite Brief an die Korinther*, KEK Sonderband, 1976

H.Conzelmann, *First Corinthians*, Hermeneia, Philadelphia 1985

E.Fascher, *Der erste Brief des Paulus an die Korinther*, ThHK VII/1, 1975

G.Friedrich, *Der erste Korintherbrief*, lectures at the University of Erlangen, winter semester 1956/57, transcribed from the notes of M.A.Bartholomäus

G.Kittel and G.Friedrich (eds.), *Theological Dictionary of the*

New Testament (1933-1979), Grand Rapids 1964ff.

F.Lang, *Die Briefe an die Korinther*, NTD 7, 1986

H.Lietzmann, *An die Korinther I/II*, HNT 9, ⁵1969

B.Reicke and L.Rost, *Biblisch-theologisches Handwörterbuch*, Göttingen 1966

W.Schrage, *Der 1.Brief an die Korinther*, EKK VII/1, 1991

A.Strobel, *Der erste Brief an die Korinther*, ZBK 6.1, 1989

J.Weiss, *Der erste Korintherbrief*, KEK V, ⁹1910

D.Wendland, *Die Briefe an die Korinther*, NTD 7, ⁹1963

U.Wilckens, *Das Neue Testament übersetzt und kommentiert*, 1970

3. Narrative interpretations

H.Frör, 'Nachtgespräch' (on I Cor.7), in *Wie eine wilde Blume, Biblische Liebesgeschichten*, 1990

W.J.Hollenweger, *Konflikt in Korinth. Memoiren eines alten Mannes: Zwei narrative Exegesen zu 1.Korinther 12–14 und Ezechiel 37*, 1978

S.Krahe, *Das riskierte Ich. Paulus aus Tarsus, Ein biografischer Roman*, 1991

C.Morris, *Epistles to the Apostle*, London 1974

4. On the understanding of religious experience

E.Etzold, *Der heilige Atem – Physiologische und psychologische Begleiterscheinungen der Glossolalie*, Materialdienst der EZW, 1, 1991

Morton Kelsey, *Trance, Ecstasy and Demons. On the Discerning of Spirits*, 1994

W.May and W.Sauter, *Ruhen im Geist*, Lüdenscheid 1990

K.G.Rey, *Gotteserlebnisse im Schnellverfahren, Suggestion als Gefahr und Charisma*, Munich 1985

A.Schosch, *Das Gift der alten Schlange?* (on charismatic renewal and speaking with tongues), Kleine Schriften-Reihe zu Zeitgeschehen no. 4, Bretzfeld 1992

C.T.Tart, *Transpersonal Psychologies*, New York 1975

Abbreviations

BBB	Bonner Biblische Beiträge
BEvTh	Beiträge zur Evangelischen Theoloige
BSt	*Biblische Studien*
BWANT	Beiträge zur Wissenschaft vom Alten und Neuen Testament
BZ	*Biblische Zeitschrift*
BZNW	Beiheft zur Zeitschrift für die Neutestamentliche Wissenschaft
EKK	Evangelisch-katholischer Kommentar zum Neuen Testament
EvTh	*Evangelische Theologie*
EZW	Evangelische Zentralstelle für Weltanschauungsfragen
FRLANT	Forschungen zur Religion und Literatur des Alten und Neuen Testaments
FS	Festschrift
HNT	Handbuch zum Neuen Testament
Jb	Jahrbuch
KEK	Kritisch-exegetischer Kommentar über das Neue Testament
KuD	*Kerygma und Dogma*
LXX	Septuagint: the Greek translation of the Old Testament, used and quoted by Jews and Christians at the time of Paul
NF	Neue Folge
NT	*Novum Testamentum. An International Quarterly for New Testament and Related Studies*
NTA	Neutestamentliche Abhandlungen
NTD	Das Neue Testament Deutsch

NTS	*New Testament Studies*
par	Parallel passages
SBM	Stuttgarter biblische Monographien
SNTU	*Studien zum Neuen Testament und seiner Umwelt*
TDNT	*Theological Dictionary of the New Testament*, ed. G.Kittel and G.Friedrich, Grand Rapids 1964ff.
ThF	Theologische Forschung. Wissenschaftliche Beiträge zur kirchlich-evangelische Lehre
ThHK	Theologischer Handkommentar zum Neuen Testament
ThLZ	*Theologische Literaturzeitung*
WMANT	Wissenschaftliche Monographien zum Alten und Neuen Testament
WuD	*Wort und Dienst. Jahrbuch der Theologischen Schule Bethel*
WUNT	Wissenschaftliche Untersuchungen zum Neuen Testament
ZBK	Zürcher Bibelkommentar
ZNW	*Zeitschrift für die neutestamentliche Wissenschaft*
ZThK	*Zeitschrift für Theologie und Kirche*

Notes

The bibliographical references are to the bibliography on pp.156f. References are by author and short title.

Introductions

1. Kuhn, *TDNT* VI, 642.

2. Hollenweger, *Konflikt*, 13ff., has portrayed 'scarlet Chloe' evocatively as a former prostitute who is socially committed. I follow Theissen, 'Schichtung', 255f., in seeing her people more as itinerant fellow workers and therefore cannot portray her as Hollenweger does. Because of this her role is more restrained. For the existence of independent businesswomen in the Roman empire cf. Thraede, 'Frauen', 76ff. In Rome, for example, women were writers, hairdressers, tailors and private secretaries; one owned a pottery (78).

3. The inscription in the paving installed by Erastos at the theatre of Corinth does not mention his father. From this Theissen, 'Schichtung', 246, concludes that Erastos was a freeman.

4. Schüssler Fiorenza, *In Memory of Her*, 170, rightly points out that the title 'deaconess' did not denote an inferior status but on the contrary a leading function; cf. the comments on *diakonia*, p.145 above.

5. For what follows see Papahatzis, *Korinth*, 19ff.; Meinardus, *Griechenland*, 71; Lang, *Korinther*, 2.

6. For economic and social conditions in the cities of the Roman empire cf. Dickey, 'Economic Conditions'; Veyne, 'Römisches Reich'; Theissen, 'Schichtung'.

7. According to Judge, 'Scholastic Community', 148ff., Paul could well have been confused with an itinerant philsopher, 'given the impression that he must have made on his contemporaries with his activities'.

1. The province of Asia comprised the Western part of Asia Minor (the territory of present-day Turkey), and the province of Achaia southern Greece. For the title 'apostle' see the Appendix, 146.

2. Seafaring began after the winter break on 5 March: Reicke and Rost, *Handwörterbuch* III, 2225.

3. In II Cor. 12.18, Paul mentions that Titus visited the church in Corinth with another 'brother'. Tychikos is inserted here for the brother, whose name is unknown. See also nn.138 and 153 below.

4. 'Church of God' was the generally accepted term used of themselves by the earliest Christian communities, Dietzfelbinger, *Berufung*, 9.

5. 'The saints', i.e. 'the holy ones', was also a term Christians used of themselves: 'According to the biblical view, whoever and whatever belongs to God is holy', Lang, *Korinther*, 16.

6. If Gaius had a villa in the style of the time, the church may have gathered in the peristyle, an inner courtyard which was partly covered by a roof, supported by pillars. Veyne, 'Römisches Reich', 339ff.

7. Teaching was one of the badly paid and less well thought of professions, Lee, 'Unrest'.

8. Cf. Acts 18.27.

9. Wilken, 'Collegia', describes philosophers and philosophical schools and their practices and teachings.

10. Apollos had studied Jewish theology in Egypt. For the theology of Apollos and its effects on the Corinthian church, cf. Sellin, 'Geheimnis'. Acts 7.22 shows that in Christian circles the wisdom of Egypt was associated with the wisdom of the Old Testament.

11. 'Godfearers' was the term used of non-Jews who joined the Jewish community without having to accept circumcision or to observe the law fully, Kuhn, *TDNT* VI, 742ff.

12. An allusion to a trial which ended with Sosthenes being beaten before Gallio's tribunal, Acts 18.12–17.

13. Cf. Mark 6.8 par. To understand the objections made to Paul earning his own living see Theissen, 'Lebensunterhalt'. Other missionaries, above all those who came from Palestine, saw not earning their own living and being dependent on the hospitality of the churches as the sign of a true apostle.

14. Cf. Matt.16.18. *Keph* (Hebrew) = *kepha* (Aramaic) = *petra*

(Greek) = rock (rocky pinnacle). For the Greeks in Corinth this name would primarily have been a translation of the Aramaic title Cephas. For the title 'Cephas' and the role that Peter played in Corinth cf. Vielhauer, 'Kephaspartei', 349. He thinks it probable that Peter himself had been in Corinth (which Lang, *Korinther*, 24, doubts) and that the Cephas party was the real cause of the conflict because of its emphasis on the 'fundamental' significance of its apostle.

15. Cf. Gal.2.10. For the history of the collection for the community in Jerusalem, which is constantly echoed in the letters to the Corinthians, I have largely adopted the findings of the research by Georgi, *Kollekte*.

16. *Maranatha*, in English 'Our Lord, come', was an Aramaic cry of prayer which was uttered at a particular point in the Lord's supper, cf. I Cor.16.22, Bornkamm, 'Worship', 170f.

17. Metalware from Corinthian workshops was exported all over the world (Theissen, 'Schichtung', 264; it included bronze mirrors). There are illustrations in Papahatzis, *Korinth*, 21.

18. 'Speaking in tongues' (glossolalia) is an ecstatic form of praying, singing, speaking in foreign languages. Maly, *Mündige Gemeinde*, 183, gives a survey of forms of the phenomenon which have historical attestation. For present-day experience of speaking with tongues cf. Etzold, *Atem*, and Schosch, *Zungenreden*.

19. In the early Christian communities there was a practice of vicarious baptism for the dead. 'It was meant to give members or relatives who had been open to the Christian message but had died before their baptism, a share in the blessing of baptism', Lang, *Korinther*, 229. In some sects this custom lasted for centuries, Lietzmann, *Korinther*, 82.

20. If the Sosthenes who is mentioned in I Cor.1.1 as one of those sending the letter is the same person as the president of the synagogue in Corinth (thus Ollrog, *Mitarbeiter*, 31), who according to Acts 18.17 was beaten before the tribunal, he probably went with Paul to Ephesus as a colleague after this event.

21. For the translation 'brothers and sisters', see 148 above.

22. This clause is added, like the word 'originally' earlier. Here Paul is summing up his view of salvation history in two compressed sentences. The division into a number of sentences and the additions are intended to make the passage easier to understand.

23. Literally – 'and you are from him in Christ Jesus'. By the use of 'are' twice the translation emphasizes that Paul is thinking about

people who have passed from 'non-being' to 'being'. Paul speaks of creation from nothing and here interprets it socially: Theissen, 'Schichtung', 233. Cf. also Rom.4.17; II Cor.5.17.

24. The Greek word *kauchasthai*, here as in many translations rendered 'boast', plays a central role in the letters to the Corinthians. However, the word 'boast' cannot express the range of meaning of this term. I use the traditional translation 'boast' only where Paul himself is quoting from the Old Testament, and elsewhere replace it with a series of other terms ('impress', 'extol', 'claim validity', and so on). Cf. the Appendix, 145.

25. In this section I Cor.2.6–16 it is striking that Paul adopts a terminology which we do not find elsewhere in his writings. So it has been conjectured that he is referring to texts, or at least to ideas and phrases, from another religious environment, for example the mysteries (Conzelmann, *First Corinthians*, 57), or predecessors of Gnosticism (Wilckens, *Neues Testament*, 568) or Hellenistic-Jewish wisdom (Sellin, 'Geheimnis', 85). The sayings are said to have been 'changed and corrected by Paul' (Käsemann, 'I Kor 2.6–26', 271, thus also Sellin, 'Geheimnis'. Theissen, *Psychological Aspects*, 363, differs). To indicate how here Paul is picking up and revising ideas from elsewhere I have attempted to reconstruct a text from the 'foreign bodies' and turn it into Chrysallis' song (31). For this I have used the following passages from I Cor.2.6–16: 'We speak wisdom to the perfect (= 'initiated') . . . We speak wisdom in mystery (v.6) . . . what no eye has seen nor ear heard . . . has arisen . . . in the heart (v.9). The Spirit searches out everything, even the depths of God (v.10) . . . we see the (things) . . . of God (v.12), We speak, . . .people of the spirit interpreting things of the spirit (or, comparing things of the spirit with things of the spirit) (v.13) . . . The person of the spirit certainly understands (judges) everything, but is grasped (judged) by no one (v.15)'. Here I can only refer to the comprehensive research by Wilckens (*Weisheit und Torheit*) and Schmithals (*Gnosis*) and the discussion of it by Bornkamm, 'Vorgeschichte', 171; Arai, 'Gegner'; Sellin, 'Geheimnis'.

26. Literally: 'But it is a matter of complete indifference to me to be investigated by you or by a human court.' The word *anakrinen* (investigate) refers to an 'official, legal "investigation" and to the legitimacy of Paul's apostolate', Vielhauer, 'Kephaspartei', 50.

27. The phrase in I Cor.4.6 has remained an enigma for translators: literally, 'that you may not learn in us that above what is

written'. I have kept the 'above' and expanded it with a phrase which makes sense.

28. Literally: 'but instructing you like my beloved children'. 'Children' (*tekna*) here does not denote being childlike, but 'descent in faith': Paul brought the gospel to the community, thus becoming the 'father' who begot it, as he explains in the following sentences.

29. Literally: 'Timothy, who is my beloved and trustworthy child in the Lord.' Here, too, 'child' means that he has come to faith through Paul: Ollrog, *Paulus*, 20 n.66.

30. Nowadays we find this judgment of Paul's difficult to take: 'The delivery of the guilty party over to Satan – which is identical with exclusion from the community . . . obviously entails the death of the guilty', Käsemann, 'Holy Law', 71. However, the aim of the judgment is the ultimate deliverance of the one who has been condemned.

31. With Strobel, *Korinther*, 101, I assume that Paul is using the impending passover as an occasion for underlining his statements with motifs from the passover, and that Timothy will arrive with the letter shortly before the festival. Lietzmann, *Korinther*, 24, and Schrage, *Korinther*, 384, differ.

32. To this point the letter is a translation of I Cor.1.1–4.8. The folowing ending has been supplied from other endings to Paul's letters (Phil.4.21–23; I Thess.5.26).

33. 'Apparently the summons to the holy kiss is the introduction to the holy meal', Bornkamm, 'Worship', 169. At the end of letters Paul often uses formulations from the eucharistic liturgy (Rom.16.16; I Thess.5.26; I Cor.16.20–24; II Cor.13.12). He presupposes that the reading of his letter will be part of the worship which ends in the ceremonial meal.

34. Hollenweger, *Konflikt*, 23ff., gives a vivid description of a baptism in the Corinthian church at dawn.

35. This formula from Gal.3.28 is regularly echoed in the New Testament in connection with baptism and is probably a baptismal saying known in the churches: Lührmann, 'Sklave oder Freier', 57; Thyen, 'Männlich und weiblich', 138; Schüssler Fiorenza, *In Memory of Her*, 205–42.

36. 'Cross' was used in Roman society as a crude swearword. For crucifixion, which is talked about in the following section as a cruel and shameful form of execution, cf. Hengel, *Crucifixion*.

37. Thus also Sellin, 'Geheimnis'.

38. Theissen, 'Die Starken', shows that the questions of the

Corinthians to which Paul refers in I Corinthians have been put one-sidedly from the perspective of the 'strong', who are to be sought among the well-to-do, and that with his answer (in the following letters) Paul too predominantly addresses the strong (169).

39. In the earliest Christian churches, passover night was celebrated as a feast of expectation of the coming Christ. The feast ended with a meal at the first cock-crow (J.Jeremias, *pascha*, *TDNT* V, 901). In 55 passover fell on the night of Sunday, 30 March (spring full moon, calculated from historical calendar dates by Reicke/Rost, *Handwörterbuch* III, 2217).

40. For Hellenistic thought the soul was the temple of the divine, Weiss, *Erste Korintherbrief*, 166; Käsemann, '1.Kor 6.19–20', 277.

41. A good century later a certain Cornelius Babbius Philinus established a temple and a monument in the forum of Corinth. I have found his name on a stone in Corinth, but not in any historical lexicon. The Babbios here could have been one of his ancestors, who had already attained power and influence in the time of Paul.

42. Lechaion is the west harbour and Kenchreai the east harbour of Corinth. See the maps on 187ff.

43. For the obligations of freemen to their former masters see Veyne, 'Römisches Reich', 90ff.; Lee, 'Unrest'.

44. For this standpoint represented in Corinth cf. Maurer, 'Ehe', 159ff., and Niederwimmer, *Mysterium*. Whereas Maurer interprets the question whether unmarried life might not be better as a reaction to the loose living of the 'strong' in Corinth, Niederwimmer presupposes a widespread ascetic tendency which he also sees represented by Paul.

45. The designation of the body as 'dirty, smelly and corruptible' comes from Mandaean tradition, Lang, *Korinther*, 785.

46. Acts 15.28f. shows that such reports were in circulation. Paul himself differs, Gal.2.6f.

47. Theissen, 'Die Starken', 61f., points out that many people were too poor to buy meat. For them, the only possibility of eating meat was at public festivals, which always involved sacrifices.

48. Corinth was known world-wide as a place of prostitution. The term *korinthiazesthai*, derived from the name of the city, was a term for visiting brothels (Friedrich, *Erster Korintherbrief*, 23f.). It is improbable that this was cultic prostitution in the temple of Aphrodite on the hill of Akro-Corinth, as was long assumed. There were temple prostitutes only the East, Conzelmann, 'Aphrodite'.

49. Women were married between the ages of thirteen and fifteen, men rather older, Thraede, 'Frauen', 56.

50. In the early church there were such 'spiritual betrothals' in which couples renounced sexual intercourse, and some exegetes conjecture that I Cor.7.25–38 refers to them, Niederwimmer, *Mysterium*, 119.

51. For Jews in Palestine and in the Diaspora, marriages with Gentiles were intolerable, because as idolaters these made the family impure, Delling, 'Heilig', 257 n. Many Jewish Christians in the Gentile Christian communities may have felt like Boaz.

52. Attempts to reverse circumcision by surgical means or to conceal it are attested as early as I Macc.1.15. However, Lührmann, 'Sklave oder Freier', 61, conjectures that such a practice was not engaged in by Christians. In his view, I Cor.7.17ff. is merely an argument: no one will have themselves circumcised or have their circumcision reversed.

53. According to Theissen, 'Schichtung', 259f., these were lawsuits which members of the church had against each other, over property or inheritances.

54. Justus, the surname of Titius, means 'the just'.

55. The beginning of the letter has been invented. The translation of I Cor.5.9–8.13 begins here.

56. I have inserted this clause to make the transition to the next topic easier.

57. Such 'catalogues of vices' were widespread in popular philosophy. In Hellenistic Judaism, too, they were adopted 'both for purposes of ethical instruction, and also for apologetic ends (catalogues of vices as "pagan trademarks")', Conzelmann, *First Corinthians*, 100f. Paul and other New Testament authors cite them as current summaries of wrong conduct, often without reflecting in detail on the 'vices' listed.

58. This passage cannot be translated unambiguously: it can also mean 'But if you can become free, make all the more loving use of it.' With Lührmann, 'Sklave oder Freier', 62; Conzelmann, Fascher and Wendland (*Korinther*), I have chosen the version which is more difficult for our values, contrary to Thyen, 'Männlich und weiblich', 158, and Schüssler Fiorenza, *In Memory of Her*, 209f.

59. Schrage, 'Welt', 138ff., identifies these verses as a quotation from apocalyptic tradition. He refers to a similar text from IV Ezra 16, which invites people to behave as strangers in the tribulations of the end time.

60. As Paul expresses himself here, it is not easy to see what is regarded as disreputable, the man sleeping with his girl-friend or leaving her untouched. It is also obscure whether the 'over-ripeness' refers to the man or the woman. Only the following instruction is clear: if someone has to force himself to continence, it is better for him to 'do what he desires' and marry his girl-friend.

61. The translation here follows the explanation of Niederwimmer, *Mysterium*, 120, in assuming that *thelema* (literally 'will') here means sexual desire. Thus also Conzelmann, *First Corinthians*, 160.

62. This section (I Cor.7.25–38) causes headaches for translators and exegetes in several respects. Who are the 'virgins' (*parthenoi*, here translated 'young people' or 'girls')? The adolescents or adults who live a continent life? And who are the people being addressed? Fathers? Betrothed? Or partners living continent lives in 'spiritual betrothals' (Niederwimmer, *Mysterium*, 119; Arndt and Gingrich, *gamizo*, 1). I am convinced by Lietzmann's analysis of the text (*Korinther*, 35), that the reference is to the young men and their brides.

63. Lang, *Korinther*, 113, conjectures Syria, where Peter also worked, as the origin of the critical enquiries: similarly Strobel, *Korinther*, 143; 'in the sphere of the earliest community'.

64. The mention of Barnabas (v.6) shows that the 'news' to which Paul is reacting in I Cor.9 relates to the meeting between the apostles, for there the two were still partners. They separated soon afterwards. For this meeting in 48 cf. Gal.2 and Acts 15. For the events from the meeting of the apostles up to the implementation of the collection see Georgi, *Kollekte*, 13ff. Hurd, *I Corinthians*, interprets the whole of I Corinthians as an attempt on Paul's part to explain to the Corinthians the changes in his theology which had been necessitated by the meeting of the apostles. However, this is contradicted by Gal.2.6f.; Paul got into difficulties precisely because he was so uncompromising.

65. For the varied use of the title 'apostle' cf. Hahn, 'Apostolat'. Cf also the notes on translation, 146.

66. Even Luke, who tends to be rather restrained about reporting conflicts in the church, clearly indicates how sharp the dispute was. 'When they had argued for a while', Acts 15.7.

67. For the various traditions about the result of the meeting between the apostles, see Paul's recollections in Gal.2.3–10 and the tradition which Luke had, Acts 15.19,28.

68. Bornkamm, 'Missionarisches Verhalten', 153, infers from I Cor. 9.19–23 that Paul was accused of characterless vacillation, ambiguity and lack of any standpoint.

69. There were distributions of meat on many occasions, e.g. at victories, funeral celebrations, electioneering, and feasts of foundations and associations. All were connected with sacrifices. Such distributions were the only way in which poor people would have a chance to eat meat. Theissen, 'Die Starke', 162.

70. I Thess.3.1–6. Cf. also the accusations against which Paul defends himself in I Thess.2.

71. For what follows cf. Acts 18.1–7. In 49, the emperor Claudius had expelled the Jews from Rome, Wilckens, Neues Testament, 459.

72. For the attempts of Christian groups to 'slip into other communities to spy out our freedom' (Gal.2.4), cf. Georgi, Kollekte, 15f.

73. For comparative historical figues for the speed of voyages see Reicke and Rost, Handwörterbuch III, 1697.

74. Translation of I Cor.9.1–11.1.

75. For an understanding of this section cf. Käsemann, 'Amor fati'.

76. At the Isthmian games which were held by the city of Corinth every two years, the victorious competitors were given a victory crown of withered celery, Meinardus, Griechenland, 94f.

77. Literally, 'spiritual food'; similarly in what follows, 'spiritual drink' and 'spiritual rock'. 'In an Old Testament context "spiritual" denotes divine origin', Lang, Korinther, 124.

78. Here Paul is interpreting events from the wandering of Israel in the wilderness (Exod.13–17; Psalm 105.39–41) as images (typoi) of baptism and eucharist. This kind of allegorical interpretation was current among Jews and Christians. For example, Jewish theologians interpreted the rock from which the water sprang as God's wisdom or manna as the word of God. Hahn, 'Abendmahls-überlieferung', 350.

79. The translation ends here. The end of the letter has been supplied from Phil.4.7; I Thess.5.27; Col.4.16; I Cor.16.20–21 and Rom.15.33.

80. Thus also Lang, Korinther, 90: 'Paul describes continence as a charisma, and not marriage as such, which is part of the creaturely order.' Similarly Conzelmann and Lietzmann.

81. Thus Fascher, Erster Korintherbrief, 182: 'The apostle knows that each person has his or her own gift from God, i.e. in complete

equality, both the unmarried and the married.' In my view I Cor.7.7 is support for this interpretation.

82. In her analysis of Gal.3.28 Schüssler Fiorenza shows the far-reaching consequences of this baptismal confession for women: 'If it was no longer circumcision but baptism that was the most important rite of initiation, then women became full members of the people of God with the same rights and duties. This generated a fundamental change, not only in their standing before God but also in their ecclesial-social status and function' (210).

83. Thyen, 'Männlich und weiblich', 146, thinks that the words 'male and female' were 'deliberately' omitted by Paul in I Cor.12.13 and similarly in the section I Cor.7.18–22, because he regarded the relationship between men and women in Corinth as problematical. Schüssler Fiorenza, *In Memory of Her*, 220, differs: she thinks it probable that in his remarks about the relationship between the sexes in I Cor.7, Paul 'had in mind the baptismal confession of Gal.3.28', and in particular also the third pair of opposites, which expressed freedom from male domination for women.

84. Theissen, *Psychological Aspects*, 162ff., argues from tomb sculptures of the time that the custom for women to wear a covering over their heads was relaxed as one moved westwards. In Asia Minor 98% of the women were veiled, in Macedonia 38% and in Rome 36%. In Corinth there were statues of women both with and without veils, and others with a head-dress worn more as decoration. According to Thraede, 'Frauen', 104ff., too, women in Western cities went about in public without a covering whereas in Tarsos, Paul's home town, strict veiling was the rule. See also the excursus in Lang, *Korinther*, 144.

85. Luke 7.36–50.

86. 'The slaves could eat what was left,' Veyne, 'Römisches Reich', 348. For the social problems in the church which corrupted the Lord's Supper cf. Bornkamm, 'Lord's Supper', and Theissen, 'Integration'. Bornkamm describes the Corinthians as sacramentalists for whom the meal had its effect regardless of how they behaved towards the other members of the church. Theissen assumes that food was brought and prepared for the 'Lord's Supper'. As a result of the saying over the bread it became the Lord's property. At the same time, however, the master of the house had already had a 'private meal' served to members of the church who came earlier. Theissen speaks of a conflict of roles: all classes took part in the Lord's supper on equal terms, but courtesy required special hospitality for the

richer members who came first.

87. After the extended opening of the letter, the translation of I Cor.11.2–34 begins here.

88. Instead of 'against the meaning of the supper', the Greek simply has the word '*anaxios*' = inappropriately' (Käsemann, 'Lord's Supper', 122). It has often been translated 'unworthily', thus making some Christians doubt whether they should go to the eucharist. Hence the explanatory paraphrase here.

89. According to Bornkamm. 'Lord's Supper', 147f., here Paul is using a liturgical formula by which unbelievers were excluded from the meal and believers admitted. He uses the formula of exclusion in its original sense in I Cor.16.22.

90. It was the general understanding in earliest Christianity that the bread gave a share in the body of Christ. Paul 'modifies this tradition to the point where participation in Jesus and his body beocmes identical with incorporation into the church as the body of Christ', Käsemann, 'Lord's Supper' 110. So 'respecting the body of Christ' means respecting the brothers and sisters – including those who come too late.

91. The translation ends here. The conclusion has been supplied on the basis of Gal.6.18 and other conclusions to Paul's letters.

92. Before his baptism Krispos was president of the synagogue, Acts 18.8. The president of the synagogue led the worship, organized the reading of scripture and the addresses and was also responsible for the building, Theissen, 'Schichtung', 236.

93. Joel 3.1; cf. Acts 2.17.

94. The beginning of the letter has been invented on the basis of Rom.1.7; I Cor.1.4–8; Gal.1.1 and Phil.1.9. The text of the letter which follows is a translation of I Cor.12.1–34.

95. The expression *peri ton pneumatikon* can mean both 'about the workings of the spirit' and 'about those filled with the spirit'. For an understanding of 'spirit' and 'working of the spirit' among the Corinthians and in Paul see Schütz, 'Charisma'; for the Christians in Corinth the spirit was the tangible power of the divine. Paul relates spirit and gifts of the spirit to individual capacities and corresponding tasks in the community. 'It is not the facticity of the supernatural but the modality of the appropriate usage which shows a charism to be authentic.'

96. Here, as in the following list, the translation puts into the plural what Paul expresses in the masculine singular: 'give to each for the use of all . . .' Since Paul presupposes charisms among both men

and women (cf. I Cor.11.5), the inclusive plural comes nearer to his meaning than the masculine singular, which nowadays is felt to exclude women.

97. Dautzenberg, '*Diakrisis*', has demonstrated that here we have a technical term from the sphere of prophecy ('*diakrisis*') which does not mean 'discerning', as it often translated, but the 'interpretation' of a prophetic saying. Prophecy took place at two levels: a prophet received a revelation, a mystery in the form of a word which he or she had heard, a vision, a dream, and communicated what had been received. Others interpreted what had been perceived in terms of the concrete situation. In all his letters Paul provides evidence that 'discerning the spirits' remained an indispensable task, quite independently of the meaning of this word. For contemporary discussion cf. Kelsey, *Trance*.

98. Literally: do not become children with the understanding, but become childlike with evil . . .

99. Many New Testament exegetes regard I Cor.14.33bff., which follows, as a later insertion, so the verses are omitted here. Lang, *Korinther*, 199f. has made a detailed investigation of the reasons for and against assuming such an assertion.

100. Deut.20.23: for Paul himself, too, before his conversion this passage must have been evidence of the reprehensibility of the Christian message: 'Someone who has been crucified, who has been touched by the curse of the law, can never be the Messiah', Dietzfelbinger, *Berufung*, 36. Cf. also Gal.3.13.

101. The curse against Jesus to which Paul refers in I Cor.12.3 can be understood as an expression of a split from and a repudiation of the earthly world. So Christians in Corinth will have seen the Jesus who fell victim to death as the embodiment of the 'fleshly' world and therefore will have 'rejected' him as the counterpart of the 'spiritual' Christ who gives life. Thus Schmithals, *Gnosis*, 117ff.; Friedrich, 'Christus', 166. Theissen, *Psychological Aspects*, 308, differs, assuming a slip of the tongue in speaking with tongues: *anathema* (= curse) instead of *maranatha* (= Our Lord, come!).

102. For this understanding of new life in the present which is experienced in the sacraments and in ecstasy and therefore no longer needs any future resurrection, cf. Stuhlmacher, 'Auferstehungs-zeugnis', 33ff.

103. Ezekiel 37.

104. From here to the end of the letter is a translation of I Cor. 15–16.

105. Here Paul uses a proverb current in his time. It comes from a play by the Greek poet Menander (341–290 BCE).

106. Literally; a 'soul body' (*soma psychikon*) is sowed and a 'spiritual body' (*some pneumatikon*) is raised. The same terms are paraphrased similarly in the next verse.

107. The following verse (I Cor.15.56) has been omitted here, as it interrupts the context. 'Verse 56 seems like an explanatory gloss' (Lang, *Korinther*, 241). In content, the statement could come from Paul (thus Lang).

108. Literally: ' . . .for these have supplied your deficiency'. Presumably a particular 'deficiency' is meant, about which only the Corinthians know: Ollrog, 'Mitarbeiter', 96ff.; Lietzmann, *Korinther*, 90.

109. Here Paul is taking up the eucharistic liturgy. This 'solemn curse' (Wilckens, *Neues Testament*, 616) presumably excluded the 'unbelievers', who had been admitted to the first part of the assembly as interested visitors. There then followed the prayer 'Maranatha', 'Our Lord, come', Bornkamm, 'Understanding of Worship', 170ff.

110. For the ideal of being untouched by pain and emotions in contemporary philosophy cf. Wilckens, *Weisheit und Torheit*, 265ff.; Schrage, 'Welt', 134. Both refer to Epictetus, a philosopher who lived somewhat later (he died in 138) but was a typical Stoic: 'Now no evil can come on me any longer, for me there are no longer any robbers, any storms; everything is peaceful, nothing touches ne (*ataraxia*). Every way, every city, every traveller, every neighbour is innocuous . . .'(quoted by Wilckens, 266). 'Not being touched' also applied to dying, since even there 'the door is open for the philosopher', i.e. he can calmly 'unite with the elements in death' (ibid.).

111. In characterizing the preachers who are described in what follows I have gone above all by Georgi, *Gegner*. Cf. further Käsemann, 'Legitimät', 34; Schmithals, *Gnosis*; Bornkamm, 'Vorgeschichte', 166; Friedrich, 'Gegner', 189ff.

112. There is no indication which churches had given the apostles letters of commendation. The places mentioned here have been chosen because they are in the wider sphere of Paul's churches and according to Rev.2 – though decades later – had to cope with problematical groups.

113. In the synagogues, Exod.19, the story of the revelation of God and the lawgiving on Sinai, was read at Pentecost (Reicke/Rost, *Handwörterbuch*, III, 1440). Exod.33; 34, the story of Moses seeing

God's glory on the mountain so that afterwards the divine radiance shone from his face, had even greater importance for Hellenistic Jewish theology. Both the apostles in Corinth and Paul are referring to this chapter in the argument over Moses. Stephen's speech in Acts 7 is an example of a Christian sermon on Moses (Georgi, *Kollekte*, 217; Friedrich, 'Gegner', 205). Some elements of this sermon have been used in what follows. However, Stephen's speech is centred on a different statement from that of the apostles in Corinth.

114. The assumption of Moses was common in Jewish theology: 'He is said to have journeyed from here to heaven, to leave this mortal life and become immortal' (thus Philo of Alexandria, a contemporary of Paul, *Life of Moses* II, 288, quoted in Georgi, *Gegner*, 157).

115. Here are two examples of the exegesis of Exod.33–34 from the contemporary theologians Philo and Josephus: Moses descends from the holy mountain and becomes a 'divine man': 'much more beautiful in his features than (at the time) when he went up, so that those who saw him were amazed and shocked. They could not look at him with their eyes for any length of time because of the glare of the sunny splendour which shone forth' (Philo, *Life of Moses* II, 69f., quoted in Georgi, *Gegner*, 240). 'Moses appeared . . . radiant and high-minded . . . the air became serene and pure when Moses descended' (Josephus, *Antiquities* III, 83ff., quoted in Georgi, *Gegner*, 262). The divine splendour which radiates from Moses also comes over the Israelites and changes them.

116. Deut.18.15. It is also quoted in Stephen's speech (Acts 7.37).

117. Cf. Mark 9.2–10 par and II Peter 1.16–19.

118. For ecstatic experiences today see May and Sauter, *Ruhen im Geist*; Kelsey, *Trance*.

119. The irritation which can be caused among Christians by different degrees of intensity in religious experience is as difficult to cope with now as it was then. One example is the article by W.McNamara, 'The Mystical Tradition of Christianity and Psychology', in Tart, *Transpersonal Psychologies*. McNamara confesses that he is a Christian and would probably also regard himself as a Christian mystic. His estimation of Christian tradition and spirituality compels my respect. He describes the 'mystical way' as 'purgation, illumination, union': 'As soon as a person has become free of the contradictory demands of his ego which consume his energies, he can truly live'. He makes a psychological distinction between 'transparent personalities' in whom, for example, the capacity to

translate an inner experience into a picture, a song or a poem is very much greater' (501) and untransparent persons to whom mystical experiences are also less accessible. And then McNamara feels the dilemma which this distinction between two classes of Christians could produce, since theologically it is very questionable. His attempt at a solution is to say that both are 'in the strict theological sense of the word mystics; phenomenologically, though only the transparent personality is a mystic'.

120. By 'worldly' and 'after the manner of the world' here and in the next letters I am attempting to get nearer to the meaning of the Greek terms *sarkikos* and *kata sarka*, literally 'fleshly' and 'after the flesh'. See the appendix, 144f.

121. After this introduction the translation of II Cor.2.14–6.13, 7.2–4 begins here.

122. Paul here uses the image of a Roman triumphal procession: the victor (God) travels in the chariot, and the prisoners (Paul and his fellow workers) go before him.

123. It is not always easy to decide who Paul is talking about when he speaks of 'us' or says 'we'. In this letter he means above all himself and his fellow workers (as can be seen from the juxtaposition of 'we' and 'you'), but sometimes he also includes the church in the 'we'. At some points he also seems to be speaking only of himself in the first person plural ('plural of modesty', Zmijewski, *Stil*, 120). The translation uses 'we' even where he probably means 'I'. Only at the end of the letter, where Paul alternates between 'we' and 'I', does the translation use the first person singular throughout.

124. Here for the first time in this letter Paul uses a term which has clearly played a part in the controversy and appears frequently in what follows: *diakonos* or *diakonia*, usually translated 'serve' and 'service'. 'Commission' seems to be the best English rendering, cf. the appendix, 145.

125. Here Paul calls the commission of Moses, in a very compressed phrase, the commission of death, and later on a 'commission of condemnation'. Behind it lies the experience that the Torah, the law of God handed down by Moses, led to the condemnation and execution of Christ. 'The Torah had done its work of destruction in Jesus', Dietzfelbinger, *Berufung*, 96. The law as Paul understood it also made Paul himself a persecutor of the community of Christ: 'It was the zeal of the law which set him against the Christians (Gal.1.13; Phil.3.5f.)', ibid., 23.

126. In Jewish theology, the stone tablets of the law were regarded as a 'letter from heaven' which God himself had written, and the 'letter' was now regarded as a symbol of the imperishability of the divine message, because it broke through the boundaries of time, Georgi, *Gegner*, 168ff.

127. The background to this argument is the Jewish view that 'before the fall God's glory (*doxa*) lay on Adam's face: in undisturbed relations with God he received God's *doxa* and reflected it. Through the fall Adam and all human beings with him (ApocMos.20f.; Rom.3.23) lost this splendour . . . After the fall, Moses is the great exception who is thought worthy of the divine splendour . . . By contrast, on Christ lies the full, imperishable splendour of God which guarantees life' . . .', Dietzfelbinger, *Berufung*, 73.

128. Here and in what follows Paul is referring to Exod.33–34, cf. n.113 above.

129. Exod.34.34: literally, 'as soon as he turns round . . .' Paul interprets the statement, which originally referred to Moses, in terms of Israel (Dietzfelbinger, *Selbstbewusstsein*, 27), of whom he can speak in the singular as the people. In an English translation what is meant becomes clearer if the reference to 'the Israelites' is brought out by the plural.

130. The motif of 'seeing in a reflection' is widespread in Hellenistic Jewish theology. There are many instances in Bultmann, *Zweiter Brief*, 93–9. Lietzmann, *Korinther*, 113f., quotes Philo, who interprets Exod.33.18 like this: 'Moses wants to see God's form . . . in a mirror but not in a created one, because the reflections seen in creation . . . pass away. God himself is to be his mirror.' So Paul is dealing with the question what kind of 'mirror' we can see God in, and what happens to us as a result. His answer is that through the spirit we look on Christ, who is the (reflected) image of God, and that changes us.

131. This word ('*syneidesis*') normally means conscience, but can also denote the 'inner authority' in a person, which also judges others as a witness, judge or observer, Eckstein, *Syneidesis*. That is how I understand it here (II Cor.4.2) and once again below (5.11).

132. Dietzfelbinger, *Berufung*, 49ff., shows that here Paul is speaking of the vision at his call before Damascus: 'Paul saw Jesus in his vision of Christ, with God's light on him; he saw him in the splendour of heavenly glorification' (63). 'God created light in him and thus brought about in him a kind of new creation which he, Paul, is to pass on in his preaching' (ibid.).

133. Paul has developed not only the content but also the form of the following verses in an artistic way (Hofius, 'Versöhnungsgedanken', 187f.). The arrangement of the text should make the structure clear and thus also make it easier to grasp the content of the compressed statements.

134. There has been much puzzlement over this statement. It is improbable that Paul is alluding to the personal acquaintance of his opponents with the earthly Jesus (thus Lietzmann, *Korinther*, 125f.). Friedrich, 'Gegner', 198; Hengel, *Crucifixion*, 70; Wilckens, *Neues Testament*, 635; and Lang, *Korinther*, 297 relate the statement to Paul's vision and thus to his hostility to Jesus at the time. In the context of the controversy the question seems to me what kind of knowledge of Christ is 'fleshly' and what really accords with Christ. Thus just as Paul's opponents dismissed his preaching as 'after the flesh' (II Cor.10.2), so Paul conversely explains their way of presenting Christ as 'fleshly', in that he is saying to the Corinthians: 'You and I no longer know Christ *kata sarka* (= after the flesh), we do not let ourselves be influenced by the mistaken relationship of this itinerant preacher with Christ', Dietzfelbinger, *Selbstbewusstsein*, 83.

135. The translation 'among us' is also possible. As Paul is talking about the foundation of his commission and not making a general statement, the meaning 'through us' (= through me and my fellow workers) is more probable; Dietzfelbinger, *Selbstbewusstsein*, 87.

136. Literally: weapons . . . to the right and to the left, i.e. offensive weapons (held in the right hand) and defensive weapons (held in the left hand).

137. Friedrich, 'Amt', 33ff., has demonstrated the artistic structure of this poem.

138. Literally: 'I speak as to children', cf. n.28.

139. The translation ends here. The conclusion has been added on the basis of other endings to Paul's letters and Num.6.25.

140. Cf. Gal.3.16.

141. Jewish-Hellenistic missionaries presented themselves to their audiences as the 'seed of Abraham', 'Israelites' and 'Hebrews'. Evidently the new apostles were Christian missionaries who came from this Jewish-Hellenistic missionary tradition and adopted its methods to win recruits for the Christian faith, Georgi, *Gegner*, 76ff. The exposition of the Torah, the law of Moses, given by God for the well-being of all humankind, remained the basis of preaching for them. They were no exceptions here. The majority of Christians saw

Jesus as the fulfilment of the Torah. Paul with his abrupt contrast with the law of Moses was in the minority, and his passion at this point was presumably understood by very few. Dietzfelbinger, *Berufung*, 90ff.

142. The Greek word for 'church' (*ekklesia*) originally means popular assembly.

143. In Acts of Paul 3, Paul is described a 'small of stature, with a bald head and bandy legs' (Rebell, *Apokryphen*, 159. However, the Acts of Paul were only written at the end of the second century, ibid., 161). That he was relatively small could be inferred from Acts 14.12, where he is given the role of Hermes alongside Barnabas as 'Zeus' (however, other reasons are given for this there). In Philemon 9 Paul calls himself an 'old man' (the letter was written at the latest five years after events in Corinth). He may have been between fifty and sixty at the time of his second visit to Corinth. It is certain that he already had more than twenty years of missionary work behind him.

144. I am grateful to Krahe, *Paulus*, 230–4, for suggestions how to describe this event. The detailed course of the visit is not known. From the subsequent of Paul it emerges only that: 1. the visit was a failure; 2. it led to insults on both sides (II Cor.1.1–4); one member of the community grossly insulted Paul, and the church let him (II Cor.2.5–11).

145. From here to the end of the letter is a translation of II Cor.10–13. The beginning is modelled on Galatians, in which Paul is engaged in just as harsh a quarrel as here: the name of the sender with emphasis on his calling by God, a brief address, the greeting expanded into a confession, praise of God, no expression of gratitude (as in all the other letters), but an immediate reference to the dispute.

146. Literally: measure of the standard (*metron tou kanonos*). The context shows that Paul is speaking of the sphere of work (= *kanon*) which God has assigned him and which extends right through the Gentile world to the end of the Mediterranean: he plans to get as far as Spain (Rom.15.28). Bultmann, *Zweiter Brief*, 195; Dietzfelbinger, *Irrlehrer*, 22.

147. Literally: 'We do not extend ourselves here like those who are not coming to you'. The meaning of the statement is uncertain.

148. The expressions 'false apostles' and further on 'false brothers' (Greek *pseudapostoloi, pseudadelphoi*), are probably composite words created by Paul himself, taking up the *pseudo-prophetai* = 'false prophets' known from the LXX (Zmijewski, *Stil*, 156, 258, 295). So I have left the terms as loan words.

149. 'In Roman fashion' is an explanatory addition. The first readers of the letter would know what kind of beating was meant without any explanation. According to Jewish law, forty strokes was the upper limit (Deut.25.1–3). For safety's sake, so as not to transgress the law, one stroke less was inflicted.

150. By the 'false brothers', Paul means those Christians who are spying out his communities, Gal.2.4, cf. 40ff. and n.72.

151. Evidently Paul is speaking of a painful bodily illness. One can only conjectures what illness he actually suffered from, e.g. epilepsy, malaria, migraine, etc.; cf. the excursuses in Lietzmann, *Korinther*, 156f.; Lang, *Korinther*, 350f.

152. Here Paul is speaking of miracles which he did in Corinth. Evidently even the sick were healed by his activity. His opponents wrongly accuse him of lacking the 'signs of an apostle', but what was inevitably offensive to them was Paul's own affliction, which seems to contradict his authority – as in the case of the crucified Jesus: 'He saved others, himself he cannot save' (Matt.27.42). Cf. here Jervell, 'Zeichen' and 'Charismatiker'.

153. No name is given here in the text as it has come to us, as in II Cor.8.18 and 22. Ollrog, 'Mitarbeiter', 52, and others conjecture a later deletion, since it is hardly explicable why Paul should omit names in this argument. Lietzmann, *Korinther*, 136, thinks in terms of one of Paul's colleagues who according to Acts 20.4 were chosen to bring the collection. Here and in II Cor.8.17 (133) I have added the name of Tychikos, in order to get nearer to the original text of the letter. Tychikos was a colleague of Paul's in Ephesus, whom Paul often 'sent' and who was one of those bringing the collection, cf. Acts 20.4; II Tim.4.9; Col.4.7; Eph.6.21.

154. 'Criticism' and 'critics' are additions which clarify one possible translation. All that is clear from the statement is that for Paul, his own competence is less important than the preservation and restoration of the community.

155. Possibly this was the imprisonment from which Paul is writing to the Philippians (Phil.1.12ff.).

156. An inscription in a paved square near the theatre of ancient Corinth indicates that a certain Erastos had the pavement installed at his own expense when he took on the office of aedile. The aediles were a kind of third and fourth mayor in Corinth. So Erastos decided to continue his political career, assuming that the Erastos who sends greetings in Rom.16.23 as a city official from Corinth is the same as the Erastos of the inscription. This is possible, but not certain.

Theissen, 'Schichtung', 242ff.

157. I have paraphrased the sentence to make it more comprehensible. Literally: 'And with this certainty I wanted to come to you that you might have a second grace.' 'Grace' (*charis*) can be understood here both in the theological sense and in a more general sense as joy, pleasure, cf. Bultmann, *Zweiter Brief*, 41f.; Lietzmann, *Korinther*, 102.

158. Baptism is paraphrased with terms like 'empower', 'anoint' and 'seal', Hahn, 'Ja', 237.

159. A free translation. Literally: 'For if I have boasted to him somewhat about you, I have not been put to shame.'

160. From the beginning of the letter to this point is a translation of II Cor.1.1–2.13; 7.5–16. The conclusion has been supplied on the basis of I Thess.5.23–24.

161. Hellenistic philosophies tended to list the 'different decrees of fate' and thus demonstrate their 'supremacy over any suffering, anxiety and fear', Zmijewski, *Stil*, 307.

162. Isa.60.5 LXX. For the interpretation of the collection as the eschatological procession of the nations to Mount Zion cf. Georgi, *Kollekte*, 72ff.

163. The city of Corinth had been rebuilt as a Roman city by Julius Caesar shortly before his death (in 44 BCE), so that the centenary of the founding of the city was celebrated in 56 or 57, Papahatzis, *Korinth*, 20.

164. The translation of II Cor.8 follows.

165. In this letter Paul deliberately uses the same word (*charis*) for God's grace and for the collective gifts of the churches. The translation attempts to do justice to this with the word 'concern'.

166. This letter is among other things a letter of commendation for two 'brothers' who are entrusted with making the collection. Remarkably enough, their names are not mentioned in the text as it has come down to us. Here, too, we are to conjecture a later deletion, as in II Cor.12.17; cf. 112 and n.153. Here similarly I have inserted Tychikos; according to Lietzmann, *Korinther*, 136, we are to assume that Paul is sending the same fellow-workers who had prepared the collection with Titus the previous year.

167. I have inserted as the name of the second brother Sosipatros, a Christian from Beroea in Macedonia, who in Rom.16.21 sends greetings from Corinth and according to Acts 20.4 was similarly one of Paul's companions on the way to Jerusalem.

168. The translation ends here. The ending of the letter has been expanded.

169. Paul wrote a similar letter on the collection to the churches in Achaia. It has been handed down in II Cor.9. This letter is only mentioned here, without the text being given. There is a detailed analysis of the two letters II Cor.8 and 9 in Betz, *Second Corinthians*.

170. II Corinthans is quoted for the first time in Marcion's writings (c. 140 CE), whereas I Clement (96 CE) refers to I Corinthians as 'the (!) letter of blessed Paul' and quotes from it. Bornkamm, 'Vorgeschichte', 188, conjectures that the letters collected in II Corinthians were edited shortly after I Clement, i.e. around 100 CE.

171. This remark relates to I Clement, a circular letter of the Roman church or its leading men to the Corinthian church, prompted by a 'rebellion' of the younger members in Corinth against the elders. 'A demand is made for the reinstatement of the presbyters . . . Possibly arbitrators were even sent to Corinth', Rebell, *Apokryphen*, 207.

172. Cf. Rom.15.21.

Appendix

1. Cf. the list of persons on pp.ixff.

2. Investigated by Theissen, 'Schichtung'.

3. For the dating see Georgi, *Kollekte*, 25ff.; Schmithals, *Gnosis*, 104ff.; Lang, *Korinther*, 14; Schrage, *Korinther*, 34ff.

4. Schmithals, *Gnosis*, 104ff., examines the possibility that all the letters were written between spring and autumn in a single year.

5. Bornkamm, 'Vorgeschichte', 171 n.66, against Schmithals.

6. Betz, *Second Corinthians*. Betz gives a comprehensive survey of the history of the theories of division in his investigation of II Cor.8–9 (3–36).

7. Bornkamm, 'Vorgeschichte'. Similarly Friedrich, 'Amt', 7; Dietzfelbinger, 'Selbstbewusstsein', 2ff.; similarly Schmithals, 'Briefsammlung', 288; and Wilckens, *Neues Testament*, 617f., who connects the 'apologia' with the 'tearful letter'. Lang, *Korinther*, 13f., sees II Cor.1–8 as a unity despite the breaks, but recognizes the second collection letter (9) and the tearful letter (10–13) as separate letters. Hyldahl, 'Einheit', and Borse, '"Tränenbrief"', 175ff., maintain the unity of II Corinthians. The latter assumes an interim report which is to explain the break between chs.9 and 10.

8. Weiss, *Erster Korintherbrief*, XL.

9. Weiss, *Erster Korintherbrief*, already put together two or three letters out of fifteen fragments. Schmithals, 'Briefsammlung', reconstructs four letters out of fifteen parts; Schenk, 'Briefsammlung', four letters out of eighteen parts; Wilckens, *Neues Testament*, 560, two letters out of nine parts; Sellin first of all ('Geheimnis', 72 n.9) three letters out of seven parts and later ('Vorbrief') three letters out of ten parts. Sellin's second attempt is attractive and worth considering because he has a plausible explanation for the redaction and also offers a solution to the question of the preliminary letter.

10. Thus Wendland, *Korinther*, 4; Lang, *Korinther*, 5; Schrage, *Korinther*, 63ff.

11. There is a summary of the reasons for the unity of I Corinthians in Schrage, *Korinther*, 63–71.

12. Schreiber, *Gruppendynamische Betrachtung*, analyses I Corinthians from the perspectives of group dynamics. His starting point, too, is the unity of the letter, i.e. he does not note any dynamic changes within the letter, but recognizes in I Corinthians as a whole a typical phase of the church process whose characteristics he discovers right through the various parts of the letter. However, the unity of the situation seems to me to be questionable from the perspective of group dynamics. Thus in my view Paul's different reactions to the demand that he should justify himself (4.3ff.; 9.1ff.) seem to point to two distinct stages of the controversy: in I Cor.4.3 Paul rejects any self-defence, whereas in 9.1ff. he justifies himself at length (and this continues even more vehemently in II Corinthians). This shows a heightening of the tensions and in my view is an indication of at least two letters and the sequence in which they were written.

13. This view is also put forward by Sellin, 'Vorbrief', 540, taking up A.Suhl (*Paulus und seine Briefe. Ein Beitrag zur paulinischen Chronologie*, StNT 11, 1975), even if he separates 5.1–8 from chs.1–4 and inserts a preliminary letter which is composed of five sections of chs.5,6,9,10 and 11.

14. Cf. Berger, 'Apostelbrief'.

15. Lang, who really cannot be said to be over-hasty in doubting the traditional text, comes to this conclusion after very careful investigation of the two passages (*Korinther*, 199f., 309ff.).

16. Lang, *Korinther*, 241, mentions the explanatory chacter of the verse (explanatory gloss) but nevertheless attributes it to Paul.

17. Betz, *Second Corinthians*, 87.

18. Zmijewski, *Stil*, 439.

19. Ibid., 414.

20. There is a wealth of references in ibid, on II Cor.11.1–12.10. I have noted many of Zmijewski's findings in the translation, but it was impossible to render others adequately.

21. Dietzfelbinger, *Irrlehrer*, 18.

22. Georgi, *Gegner*, 31ff.

23. So also Ollrog, 'Mitarbeiter', 68.

24. For the different meanings of *apostolos* see Hahn, 'Apostolat'.

25. Dietzfelbinger, *Berufung*, 66.

26. Friedrich, 'Christus', 152f.

27. Arndt and Gingrich, *Lexicon*, 'en', 5 d.

28. Ibid., s.v. '*adelphos*'.

Maps

Corinth in the Time of Paul

Based on Scranton, *Kenchreai*, Outlines 1 and 2, and Papahatzis, *Korinth*, 8f., 13 and 49.

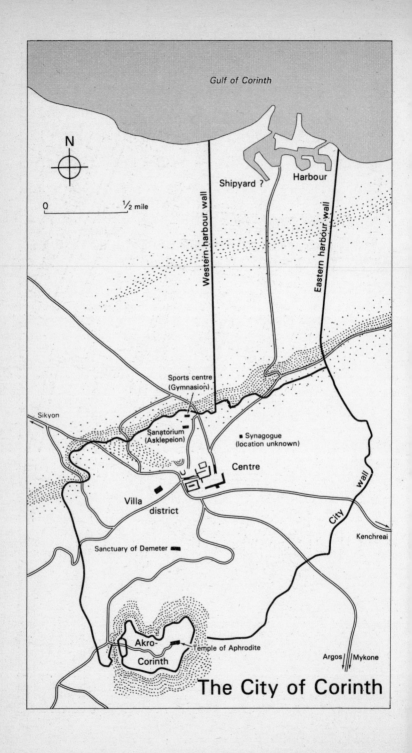

The City of Corinth

City Centre (Excavations)

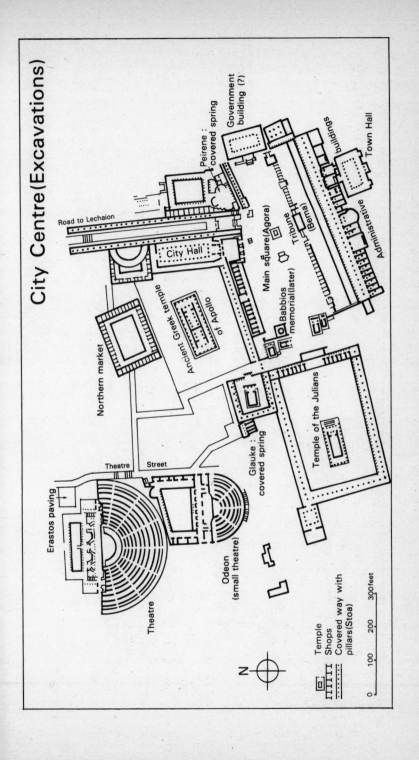

Road to Lechaion

Peirene : covered spring

Government building (?)

Town Hall

Administrative buildings

Main square (Agora)

Tribune (Bema)

Babbios memorial (later)

City Hall

Ancient Greek temple of Apollo

Northern market

Glauke : covered spring

Temple of the Julians

Theatre Street

Erastos paving

Theatre

Odeon (small theatre)

N

Temple
Shops
Covered way with pillars (Stoa)

0   100   200   300 feet

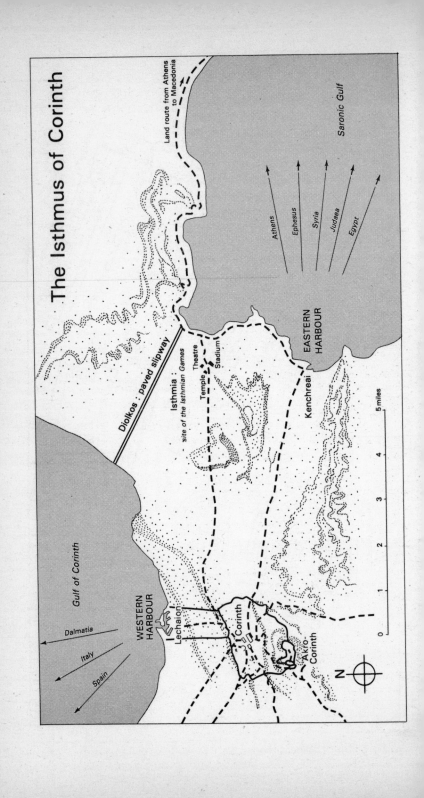

The Isthmus of Corinth